Collins

Revised

Engaging English 8

Preeti Roychoudhury
Sadeqa Rahman Siddiqui

Components of DigiSuite

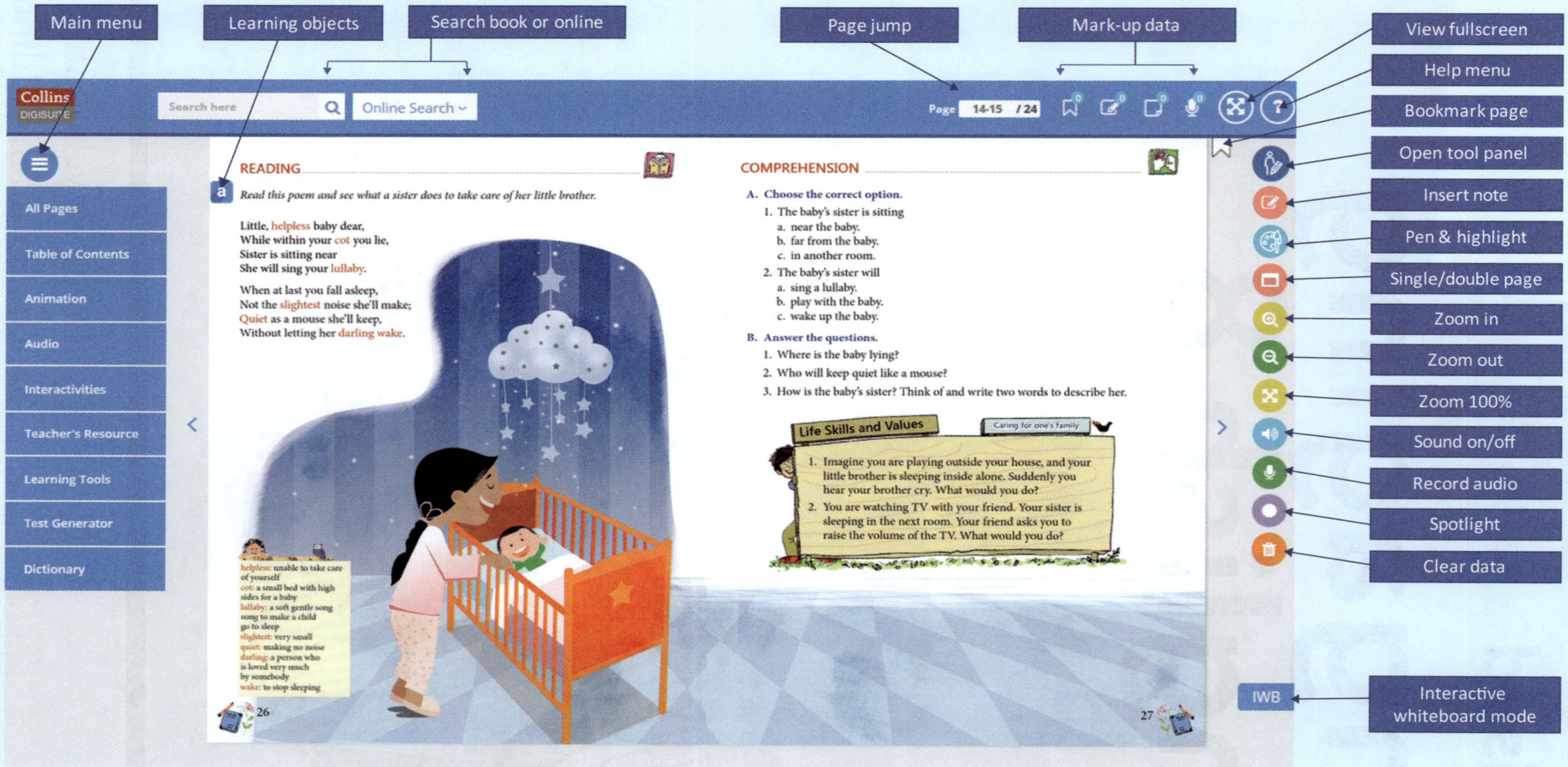

Student + Teacher			Teacher-only	
a animations	ia activities	g games	lp lesson plans	tn teacher's notes
ilt instructor-led tutorials	w worksheets	v videos	w worksheets	ak answer keys
	audio			

Preface

Revised Engaging English aims to instill an appreciation for literature in today's learners, while equipping them with the tools to develop native fluency and communicative competence in using the English language.

This eight-level series has been designed to teach language skills through the use of literature. Comprising Coursebooks and Workbooks, and digital resources for teachers for all levels, the series is meant to be educative as well as inspiring, imparting moral values and arousing the learner's curiosity about the world beyond the classroom.

In the revised edition, the series has been aligned closely with the guidelines of the National Education Policy, 2020 through its focus on twenty-first century skills, Sustainable Development Goals (SDGs), cross-curricular learning, 'Happiness' content and art-integrated learning. Coursebooks 1 and 2 integrate the essence of NIPUN (National Initiative for Proficiency in Reading with Understanding and Numeracy), which deals with Foundational Literacy and Numeracy. They aim to motivate students to read independently, improve their vocabulary, develop their critical thinking and creative skills and enhance their ability to express themselves verbally and in writing.

The lessons are built around carefully selected literary pieces with distinct cross-curricular themes, and presented with glossary, explanation of literary terms and interesting trivia. The end-of-chapter exercises address the needs of formal language learning and cover all aspects of language acquisition. They include *Comprehension, Way with Words, Grammar in Use, Study Skills, Listening and Speaking* and *Pen it Down*.

New Features in the Revised Edition

Let's Get Started: A theme-based, cross-curricular warm-up task at the beginning of each lesson spanning subjects like science, history and general knowledge, with a focus on SDGs.

Graphic stories: These include both fiction and non-fiction and address the needs of visual learners.

Cross-curricular trivia: This includes **Did You Know?**, which has interesting information covering science, mathematics, geography, history and general knowledge, related to the passage.

In-text questions: These assess while-reading comprehension of the learner.

Life Skills and Values: A part of Comprehension, this includes questions that encourage learners to think analytically and write creatively, thus building higher order thinking skills. They are aligned to the twenty-first century skills.

Augmented scaffolding: This comprises more detailed explanations for every section, including Way with Words and Grammar in Use. Concepts are presented through graphic organizers and reinforced through practice and repetition. Support is provided for the Listening and Speaking and Pen it Down tasks in the form of suggested points as well as useful words and phrases to facilitate competency-based learning.

Now I can: This is a learner-centric self-assessment checklist of the learning objectives for every lesson.

Be Creative!/Research and Write: These special pages, of which there are three in each book, include several new research-based literary projects, creative writing and vocabulary tasks which revisit the themes of the lessons. These focus variously on art integration and SDGs and support inquiry-based learning.

The **Workbooks** complement the Coursebooks by providing additional skills practice through the careful mapping of grammar and vocabulary. Each Workbook from Classes 3 to 8 includes a test paper based on the principle of SAFAL (Structured Assessment For Analyzing Learning), a competency-based assessment introduced by CBSE in keeping with the guidelines of the NEP. They focus on assessing the competencies of critical thinking as well as inquiry-based and analysis-based learning.

The series is supported with **Teacher's Resource Books** and **Digital resources**.

The series encourages competency-based education which allows concept acquisition at the learner's own pace, based on individual ability. We hope that it will foster a love for literature and reading in young learners.

Authors

Preeti Roychoudhury has taught English for over two decades at various schools, including Loreto House, Kolkata and Calcutta International School.

Sadeqa Rahman Siddiqui has been teaching English for a decade at La Martiniere for Boys, Kolkata.

Key Features

Let's Get Started

- Theme-based warm-up activities, with a focus on Sustainable Development Goals

Reading

- Has a rich variety of reading passages, including prose, poetry and drama
- Covers literary genres like short stories, biographies, folktales, fables, fantasy, science fiction, non-fiction, extracts from contemporary and classic works, taken from Indian and world literature

Introduction

- Includes background information about the reading text to initiate learners into the passage

Wordwise

- Provides additional information on the origin of words to interest learners in the nuances of language and to improve vocabulary

In-text questions

- 'while-reading' questions to check textual understanding

Comprehension

- 'Quick Recap' checks factual understanding through 'who', 'what', 'where', and 'how' questions; also includes 'reference to context' questions to test in-depth understanding of the lesson

Life Skills and Values

- Inferential and extrapolative higher order thinking skills (HOTS) questions on moral values and interpersonal skills, mapped to twenty-first century skills

Graphic Story

- Graphic story in Classes 1-7 to aid visual learning

Glossary

- Provides contextual meanings of difficult words and phrases, given alongside the reading passage

About the author/poet

- Gives a brief biography of the writer, with names of their best known works

Literary term, Did You Know?

- Provide additional information on literary devices and figures of speech, and trivia to develop cross-curricular intelligence

Way with Words

- Includes exercises on contextual application of language encountered in the reading text
- Fosters appreciation of literary devices and figures of speech (simile, metaphor, personification, etc)

Grammar in Use

- Imparts formal understanding of language structures and syntax
- Includes easy-to-understand explanations of grammar concepts, graphic organisers and plenty of practice exercises

Listening and Speaking

- Facilitates fluency in oral and aural communication
- Includes conversation practice, role plays, debates and listening comprehension
- Exercises on rhyme and meter in poetry chapters

Pen it Down

- Includes guided and free writing tasks, to enable learners to express themselves creatively, logically and coherently

Now I can

- Self-assessment of learning objectives for the chapter

Study Skills

- Develops the sub-skills of language study
- **Spell Check** and **Pronounce Well** include phonics drills and exercises on spelling
- **Use Your Dictionary** develops dictionary referencing skills

Literary Genres and Terms

- Includes a glossary to introduce literary genres and explain literary devices and narrative tools

Read More

- Contains extra suggested reading for the avid learner to foster love for literature

Assessments

- Includes a Test Paper in Workbooks 3-8 based on the principle of SAFAL that encourages competency-based learning

Poster

- Literature and vocabulary games, and activities based on distinct themes

Icons

Revised Engaging English aims to equip students with various skills outlined in the National Education Policy, 2020, that target the holistic education of the learner. Take a look at the various icons used to showcase these skills.

Twenty-first Century Skills

Mastering these skills will equip learners to face the challenges of a rapidly changing, digital society.

Happiness Content

The idea underlying 'Happiness Content', a part of the 'Happiness Curriculum', is that learning should be an enjoyable process. For knowledge to bring joy, learning must focus on concept-based rather than rote learning.

1 HC **Learning and Awareness**

Exploring happiness through Learning and Awareness

2 HC **Feelings**

Experiencing happiness in relationships through Feelings

3 HC **Active Participation**

Happiness through Active Participation

The Sustainable Development Goals (SDGs) were adopted by the United Nations in 2015 as a universal call to action to end poverty, protect the planet, and ensure that by 2030, all people enjoy peace and prosperity. The 17 SDGs recognize that development must balance social, economic and environmental sustainability.

Art Integration

The arts, or the fine arts, are painting, sculpture, architecture, poetry, music, literature and dance. Art-integrated experiential learning uses concepts from the arts to provide learners a multi-disciplinary experience.

Cross-curricular Content

The cross-curricular approach to teaching recognises that subjects are inter-linked, and for effective concept-acquisition, they must be taught in synergy with each other.

Acknowledgements

The publishers wish to thank and acknowledge the following for granting us permission to use copyright material:

Adithi Rao for *The River Came Home* (from *Growing Up in Pandupur*). Published by Zubaan. Reprinted with the permission of the author; Ranju Dodum for *The Monk Protectors of Arunachal's Wetlands*, taken from the Mongabay article *https://india.mongabay.com/2021/03/the-monks-who-protect-the-bhagajang-wetland/*, reprinted with the permission of the author; 'The Commentator' from *Song of the City* by Gareth Owen. Copyright ©Gareth Owen. Reproduced by permission of the author c/o Rogers, Coleridge & White Ltd., 20 Powis Mews, London W 11 1JN; *A Short Walk in the Hindu Kush* by Eric Newby. Reprinted with permission of HarperCollins *Publishers* Ltd ©2010, Eric Newby.

The publishers have applied for permission for the following:
Felling of the Banyan Tree by Dilip Chitre, *A Tale of Two Cities* by Charles Dickens (abridged version by A. Johnson, G. C. Thornley), *The Last Wolf* by Mary TallMountain, *Refugee Blues* by W. H. Auden.
Acknowledgements for these texts will be made in the future editions of the book.

Every effort has been made to trace copyright holders and to obtain their permission for the use of copyright material. However, in some instances, we have been unable to trace the owners of the copyright pieces published here. The authors and publishers will gladly receive any information enabling them to rectify any error or omission in subsequent editions.

Illustrations

Inside: **Page 6: SDG logo and icons:** https://www.un.org/sustainabledevelopment/
The content of this publication has not been approved by the United Nations and does not reflect the views of the United Nations or its officials or Member States. **11:** Iuliia Konovaliuk; **12:** Natalie, johnwoodcock, tachyglossus, dedMazay; **13:** Benjavisa; **15:** RLTImages; **16:** mi007; sabelskaya; **17:** aqabiz; **24:** Igor Petrovic; **25:** hisa nishiya; **26:** Aleksei Morozov; **28:** artisticco; **29:** The India Today Group; **30:** beastfromeast; **34:** TAW4, MHJ; **47:** Oleksandr Pupko; **51:** IconicBestiary; **62:** mervin07, Getty Images, Keith Lance; **63:** stock shoppe, YuliiaHrozian; **66:** Zubada; **67:** ekolara; **70:** aqabiz; **71:** Kowsick Borgohain, sabirmallick; **72:** Ranjan Basu; **74:** jarino47, AYImages, RichLindie, Christophe Lehenaff; **76:** wissanu99; **78:** bagira22; **87:** larryrains; **90:** skeeg; **97:** lemono; **99:** DanielVilleneuve; **110:** Malchev; **117:** im a photographer and an artist; **118:** Mashot; **126:** Jane Semina; **128:** nizha2, ugniz, abzerit, rusm, coffeekai; **143:** Frank Bienewald; **144:** ajijchan; **159:** HSStyle; **161:** fractalgr; **170:** Malchev; **171:** Ponomariova_Maria; vectorikart; **172:** ODD ANDERSEN, duncan1890; **173:** Getty Images.

Detailed Contents

Unit	Theme	Comprehension	Way with Words	Grammar in Use	Study Skills	Listening and Speaking	Pen it Down
11. The Six Napoleons	Mystery and Detection	• Sequencing • Reference to context	• Words from detective fiction • Types of books	• Direct and indirect speech	• Pronounce Well: *schwa* sound	• Listening comprehension: multiple choice questions, true/false	• Story writing
12. The Commentator	Sport	• Reference to context • Questions	• Idioms with *talk* • Words related to football	• Tenses	• Use Your Dictionary: headwords	• Conversation: making an apology	• Making a poster • Paragraph writing
Research and Write							
13. The Gift of the Magi	Love and Sacrifice	• Questions • Reference to context	• Idioms related to money • Suffixes	• Using *for*, *during* and *while* • Question tags • Subordinating conjunctions	• Use Your Dictionary: multi-word entries	• Listening comprehension: answering questions	• Reviewing a story • Writing an alternate ending to a story
14. The Last Wolf	Man and Nature	• Questions • Reference to context	• Contextual usage • Idioms related to wolves	• Joining sentences: participles	• Pronounce Well: the letter *u*	• Class discussion on a given topic	• Report writing
15. A Short Walk in the Hindu Kush	In Faraway Lands	• Questions • Reference to context	• Word meanings • Compound adjectives	• Joining sentences: infinitives and gerunds	• Spell Check: double consonants	• Enacting a conversation	• Picture composition
16. Refugee Blues	War and Peace	• Questions • Reference to context	• Words related to the Holocaust • Using suffixes to form nationalities	• Determiners: quantifiers and distributives • Punctuation: parentheses, ellipsis and hyphen	• Pronounce Well: diphthongs	• Listening comprehension: true/false	• Writing a poem
17. My Financial Career	Humour	• True/false • Reference to context • Character sketch	• Idioms related to anxiety • Similar sounding words	• Transformation of sentences	• Use Your Dictionary: eponyms	• Listening comprehension: multiple choice questions	• Process writing
18. The Tragedy of Julius Caesar	Ancient History	• Questions • Reference to context	• Irony • Rewriting archaic sentences	• Sentences: simple, compound, and complex • Joining sentences with correlative conjunctions	• Use Your Dictionary: Shakespearean words • Pronounce Well: stressed words in a sentence	• Enacting a scene from a play	• Writing a speech • Writing a notice
Research and Write							
Literary Genres and Terms							

Contents

free verse

1

Where the Mind is Without Fear

Rabindranath Tagore

Let's Get Started

The United Nations Sustainable Development Goal 16 promotes building of effective institutions at all levels. We should start with our schools, making them safe spaces for everyone. This would help the students grow up to be responsible and sensitive citizens.

Bullying is one of the most common problems in schools. Prepare a bullying meter with the following actions graded in it, based on the impact caused on a person (green: least impactful, red: most hurtful). You may add one action each to both ends of the scale.

- sarcasm
- hate speech
- practical jokes
- rumours
- name-calling
- hitting
- taking things by force

Suggest two ways to reduce these instances of bullying in schools.

HC **Learning and Awareness:** Understanding our desire for clarity, prosperity and coexistence in society and nature

Reading

This poem, a part of the Nobel Prize-winning collection,* Gitanjali*, was written before India won independence. It was translated from Bengali to English by Tagore himself. The poem describes his vision of a free India.

Where the mind is without fear and the head is held high;
Where knowledge is free;
Where[1] the world has not been broken up into **fragments**
By narrow domestic walls;[2]
Where words come out from the depth of truth;
Where tireless **striving** stretches its arms towards perfection;

Where the clear stream of **reason** has not lost its way
Into the **dreary** desert sand of dead habit;[3]
Where the mind is led forward by thee
Into ever-widening thought and action;
Into that heaven of freedom, my Father, let my country awake.

What should we tirelessly strive for?

Literary terms

1. This is an example of **repetition**. The poet repeats the word 'where' to keep our attention focused on his vision of a dream nation.

2. This line is an example of **imagery**. The world is being imagined as a land divided by man-made barriers, where people cannot move freely.

3. This is a **metaphor**. The ability to reason is being compared to a stream, while habit is compared to a sandy desert where the stream dries up. The poet hopes that original thinking is not forgotten because of the old ways of doing things.

fragments: small parts broken off from something

reason: (here) the ability to think and act logically

striving: trying hard

dreary: dull or lifeless

About the poet

Rabindranath Tagore (1861–1941) was a Bengali poet, novelist, painter and educator, well-known for his innovations in modern Indian art and music. He was the first Asian to receive the Nobel Prize in Literature, in 1913. He composed India's national anthem. Some of his best-known works are 'The Postmaster', *Gora* and 'Broken Nest'.

Comprehension

Quick Recap

A. Answer the questions in a few lines.

1. What do you understand by the line 'Where knowledge is free'?
2. Why would the poet's ideal country be a 'heaven of freedom'?
3. What is the figure of speech used in the line 'Where tireless striving ...'? Explain it in your own words.
4. What does the poet mean by the phrase 'let my country awake'? What state was the country in earlier?
5. Who do you think the poem is addressed to?

B. Answer the questions with reference to context.

1. *Where the world has not been broken up into fragments/By narrow domestic walls;*
   a. What do 'narrow domestic walls' represent?
   b. How do these walls reduce the world into 'fragments'?
   c. What kind of world would we have if these walls did not exist?
2. *Where the mind is led forward by thee/Into ever-widening thought and action;*
   a. Whose mind is being referred to here?
   b. Who is being addressed as 'thee'? What role does the poet wish 'thee' to play?
   c. What does the phrase 'ever-widening thought and action' mean?

Life Skills and Values — being a responsible citizen

Think and answer.

1. What fear does the poet refer to in the opening line?
2. Do you think the ideas expressed in the poem hold true in today's world? Give reasons for your answer.
3. A country is made up of the people who live in it. Identify and explain the lines in which the poet refers to the qualities of the individual who would be a part of his ideal nation.

21st Century Critical Thinking

Way with Words

Homographs and Homophones

You have studied about homographs and homophones.

Homographs are words that have the same spelling but different meanings. They are sometimes pronounced differently.

Example: bow

1. a weapon for shooting arrows or a knot tied with two loops (rhymes with *low*)
2. bend the head or upper part of the body as a sign of respect (rhymes with *cow*)

Homophones are words with the same pronunciation which may have different spellings and meanings.

Examples: two/too, maid/made

A. Write a homophone or homograph for each of these words from the poem. Then, make sentences of your own with each set of words. One is done for you.

1. *way*
   *The **way** to the castle is through a narrow marketplace.*
   *This is the right **way** to solve the problem.*

2. head	4. let	6. habit	8. where	10. been
3. led	5. arms	7. stream	9. desert	11. mind

Metaphors

B. You came across metaphors in the poem. Identify and explain the metaphors in the following sentences.

1. India is a melting pot of various cultures.
2. The poet weaves a tapestry of a dream country with his words.
3. A man's conscience is his compass.
4. He is a diamond in the rough.
5. The king's advisor turned out to be a wolf in lion's skin.
6. All the world's a stage, and men and women are actors who enter and leave.

Grammar in Use

Order of Adjectives

If there are several adjectives describing a single noun, they are placed in the following order:

Quantity → Opinion → Size → Age → Colour → Origin → Material → Purpose

Example: **Some strange small ancient brown clay cooking** pots were found under a mound in the desert.

A. Complete the sentences with the correct order of adjectives.

1. Jyoti wore a ________________ sari to the wedding.
   (blue Kanjeevaram silk/silk Kanjeevaram blue/Kanjeevaram blue silk)

2. Aunt Tarla is ________________ lady. (an old sweet/a sweet old/a sweet, old)
3. The actor who portrayed Macbeth was ________________.
(dark, handsome and tall/handsome, tall and dark/tall, dark and handsome)
4. The housing complex has ________________ buildings.
(new three five-storeyed/three new five-storeyed/five-storeyed three new)
5. The children were playing with ________________ marbles.
(some shiny, black/shiny, black some/some black, shiny)
6. You should always have ________________ vegetables with your lunch.
(some leafy, green/some green leafy/green, leafy, some)

Relative Pronouns

You know that a **relative pronoun** refers to a noun mentioned before it. We use relative pronouns (**who**, **whom**, **whose**, **which**, **that**) to join sentences.

Examples: 1. The poet has a vision of a world. This world has not been broken up into fragments. → The poet has a vision of a world **which** has not been broken up into fragments.
2. She is a helpful girl. Everyone likes her. → She is a helpful girl **whom** everyone likes.
3. This is the painting. Soumya made it. → This is the painting **that** Soumya made.

B. Join the sentences using suitable relative pronouns.

1. He was my best friend. I will never forget him.
2. That is the road. It leads to the village school.
3. Have you met Ruskin Bond? His stories are loved by children and adults alike.
4. My grandfather did not have any formal degree. He went on to become very successful in life.
5. She is the candidate. They want to hire her.
6. This is the Sanyal family. Their donations support a child welfare organisation.
7. The athlete was running at great speed. She broke the world record.

Study Skills

Spell Check

There are many ways of spelling soft 'g'. We can spell it with the letters **j**, **g** or **dg**.
Examples: **j**ustice, pa**g**e, ba**dg**e

Underline the incorrect spellings in these words pronounced with soft 'g' and correct them.

1. full-fleged
2. foliadge
3. acknowledge
4. gigsaw
5. jemstone
6. doje
7. jel
8. gingle
9. lejer
10. gist
11. gauge
12. smuje
13. generous
14. slege
15. signaje

Listening and Speaking

Listen to an excerpt from a well-known speech on freedom. Then, work in pairs to discuss the different kinds of freedom Tagore talks about in his poem. Ask your partner and share your own ideas about what freedom means to you. You can include examples of your experiences at home and school.

Present your ideas as a five-minute speech before the class.

Pen it Down

What is your vision of an ideal India? What would you like to see happening in your country in the next five years? Write an essay on the topic, giving it a suitable title.

These are some of the points you can cover in your essay:

- improvement in the condition of the poor and the underprivileged
- education for all and more employment opportunities
- more freedom of expression
- gender equality

Self Assessment

Now I can

- appreciate the poet's dream of an ideal country.
- understand the use of repetition, imagery and metaphor in the poem.
- differentiate between homophones and homographs, follow the order of adjectives and join sentences using relative pronouns.
- give a speech and write an essay on a given topic.

Read More

Democracy: In this poem, Langston Hughes says that true democracy can arrive only when people themselves are free.

If: This well-known inspirational poem by Rudyard Kipling says that an ideal human being is one who can face difficult times with a smile on his/her face.

2

The River Came Home

Adithi Rao

Let's Get Started

The United Nations Sustainable Developmental Goal 11 states that cities and other human settlements should be made safe and sustainable. Sustainability includes protecting the environment around us so that it nurtures us too.

Read this list of questions carefully and think and write the answers.

Are there enough trees in your locality?	
What are the sources of water there?	
Are there any schools nearby?	
Are there parks for children to play in your area?	
Is your locality clean and free of plastic waste?	

Share your answers with the class. Also, take turns to speak for two minutes each about the changes you would like to see in your locality that would make it environmentally sustainable.

HC **Feelings:** Contribution in others' lives

Reading

Dam-building projects have displaced people from entire villages in our country, in the past. How do young people cope with the loss of home and sudden poverty? This story is about Gopala, who is in a similar situation. It is taken from the book* Growing Up in Pandupur, *a collection of stories set in a fictitious little Indian town.

Gopala was a quiet fellow. He kept away from the other children in school, preferring to stick with his small group of friends who came from the other side of Pandupur. They travelled together to school in a rusty mini-van that **hurtled** down the street honking loudly, scattering chickens, pedestrians and cyclists.

Gopala and his friends attended Saraswati Vidyashala, but they didn't really belong there. They never played with the other children, laughed or joked or handed out toffees on their birthdays. They only spoke when spoken to and then very little.

This was the way it was, until the day Gopala got into trouble.

His friend Ananta's mother had managed to save money for a **beyblade** for her son. It was a matter of general pride and interest to the whole group.

They were unusually **animated** in class that day, to the surprise of Mani Sir, their English teacher, who had to tell them to be quiet and pay attention to the lesson. He felt uncomfortable doing this, because they instantly fell silent for the rest of the lesson. Children are naughty. Talkative. **Boisterous**. These children were none of those.

After school, Gopala and his gang made their way to Jolly Toys in downtown Pandupur. They chattered away in the local language, a gleam in their usually downcast eyes. The proprietor, Mr Kirtan, kept all kinds of toys. His biggest customers were the engineers' children from Stoney Hill High School, with their **incessant** demands for **PlayStations** and **Game Boys**.

Three boys from Stoney Hill were already in the shop, briskly examining and rejecting toys. Gopala's gang arrived and spotted a beyblade lying on top of the pile of rejects.

Ananta hurried forward and picked it up. It was beautiful. Red, shiny red, with swirls of blue and yellow!

'I'm buying that,' said a voice.

hurtled: moved fast in one direction

beyblade: a spinning-top toy originally from Japan that is popular among young adults

animated: energetic

boisterous: noisy and energetic

incessant: never stopping

PlayStations, Game Boys: popular but expensive video game brands that include hand-held video consoles

Did You Know? Geography

Pandupur is based on a small, scenic town called Pandavpur, located between Bengaluru and Mysuru.

Which school did Gopala attend?

Ananta and his gang glanced around. Sunil, the boy who spoke, said impatiently to his friend, 'I don't know the local language. How do I explain it to these chaps?'

'We can follow. We are knowing English,' Gopala said with quiet dignity.

'Good for you,' replied Sunil indifferently, extending his hand for the beyblade.

smirked: smiled in a superior way

dismissively: without giving much importance

reeled: moved in an unsteady way

bristled: became angry

intervention: coming in between

Nobody noticed Mani Sir enter the store. He had come to buy his nephew a present. Unaware that his teacher was watching him from across the store, Gopala said, 'You threw it to side.'

Sunil **smirked**. 'No, I *put* it aside to buy it.'

'So you were thinking to buy *all* those toys in that pile?' asked Gopala calmly.

Sunil turned away **dismissively** and said, 'Mr Kirtan, I'll take this beyblade and those computer games.'

Mr Kirtan smiled uncomfortably. 'Er, I only have one beyblade at the moment. Shall I put in an order for another one? Same colours if you like.'

'No, I'll take that one.'

Ananta's hand tightened over the toy. Mr Kirtan looked at Ananta. 'I'll put in an order for you boys, then.'

'We're buying this one. How much, Uncle?' asked Gopala.

Sunil turned red. 'If you sell that beyblade to those villagers, I'll make sure my friends and I never buy stuff from you.'

A fist shot out and hit him in the face. Sunil **reeled** backwards. His friends **bristled**. Only the **intervention** of Mani Sir prevented a full-fledged fight.

The next day, Mani Sir discovered that Gopala had been suspended from school for a week.

What punishment had been meted out to Gopala?

'But was it such a big deal?' he asked. 'Boys fight all the time.'

The Hindi teacher shrugged in reply.

The violence was wrong, but Gopala had certainly been **provoked**. Mani Sir had a feeling that there was something more to Gopala's sudden outburst.

After lunch, Mani Sir excused himself to the Principal and rode out on his scooter, heading west towards the dam project. Gradually, the setting became rural. At a **fork** in the road, he consulted the directions to Gopala's house that he had persuaded a nervous Ananta to give him.

Mani Sir chose the left fork and finally reached a settlement, which ironically, looked distinctly unsettled. The houses and stores were makeshift, made from tin and asbestos, instead of brick and mortar. He found Gopala's house and knocked. A woman appeared at the door.

What did the settlement look like?

provoked: caused to act in a certain way out of anger

fork: (here) divide

wary: watchful, cautious

apparent: obvious

'*Namaskara*, Ma. Are you Gopala's mother?' asked Mani Sir in the local language, folding his palms in greeting.

She nodded, looking **wary**.

'I'm Gopala's English teacher.'

The mother looked fearful. 'Is there any more trouble?'

'No, nothing like that. May I come in?'

She stepped aside to let Mani Sir enter. He sat down on the straw mat she spread for him, looked up and smiled. 'I came to tell you that Gopala has never given me or any of his teachers any trouble.'

The mother's jaw dropped open in surprise.

'Then why ...?'

The question hung in the air, the mother's sadness and confusion **apparent** in it.

'If the school hadn't suspended him, the other boy's parents would have gone to the police and made things worse for Gopala. But I was there when the fight took place. The other boy was in the wrong, not Gopala.'

The mother suddenly broke down. She wiped her eyes, blew her nose on the end of her crumpled sari *pallu* and looked up.

'There is no wrong or right, Sir. Only people with money and those without. My Gopala is finished.'

Mani Sir was startled. 'What do you mean by finished? It is not that bad. Surely you understand that?'

'I don't mean in school. I mean because he was already so sad. All our children are. And now, they will become even sadder, smile even less.'

Mani Sir watched her closely for a moment. 'Ma, I have shifted to Pandupur only this year. I'm not sure what is going on here, but Gopala and his friends seem different from the other children at school. Can you tell me why?'

'They have become like this ever since we were made to leave our homes and come here. The dam sent the river into our homes and spoiled everything. The children feel lost now. They are angry. Our home on the river bank was beautiful, Sir. We had fruit orchards and sugarcane fields. Our houses kept us warm in winter and cool in summer. Now, the roof burns in the hot season and in the cold, it is like sleeping under the freezing sky.'

Mani Sir listened in silence. Then, he stood up, having come to a decision.

'Where is Gopala, Ma?'

The woman was alarmed. 'He won't talk to anyone. Since his father beat him yesterday, he hasn't said a word.'

Mani Sir closed his eyes in despair. The last thing the boy needed was a beating.

'Still,' he said firmly, 'I want to speak to him. Please tell me where he is.'

'Probably down by the river where our homes once were. That's where he goes all the time. But ...' she trailed off anxiously.

'Don't worry,' said Mani Sir, 'I won't hurt the boy.'

There it was, that watery place where the river had swollen and swallowed up the land. It was a beautiful sight, really. A great unmoving blanket of water[1] from which the thick stump of a dead tree pointed up to the sky like an accusing finger. On top of it sat a bird of prey, waiting. And on this side of the bank sat a bowed figure, looking silently out at the waters. Gopala.

Literary term

1. This is a **metaphor**. The surface of the water is being imagined as a blanket.

Mani Sir slowly approached. 'What tree was that?' he asked conversationally. Gopala spun around and stared up at his teacher, whose eyes were far away.

'Tamarind.'

Mani Sir sat down beside him.

'Did you know it?'

'It was in our backyard.'

What were the two trees mentioned by Gopala and his teacher?

'I knew a tree once. A guava tree. When I was small, I thought it was very tall. Before they cut it down last year, I went to visit it one last time.' Mani Sir chuckled. 'It was still very tall.'

Gopala watched him curiously. 'You didn't mind that they cut down your tree?'

'I did.'

'Couldn't you stop them?'

'No.'

Gopala turned away. 'Neither could I,' he said, almost to himself.

'But there is something you can do,' said Mani Sir cheerfully.

Gopala frowned. What could he possibly do, now that his tree was dead? Mani Sir didn't offer any ideas, but continued to look at Gopala with bright, expectant eyes. And suddenly it came to him.

Gopala stood up and stripped down to his shorts. He picked up a sharp stone. For the first time since Mani Sir had set eyes on the boy, there was animation in him. Gopala dived into the water, making a splash, soaking his teacher who followed him to the water's edge.

With sure, strong strokes Gopala cut his way through the river until he reached the tree stump. Winding his left arm around it, he carved something into the trunk:

'Gopala climbed this tree.'

As Gopala turned to swim back, from across the distance, Mani Sir saw him smile.

About the author

Adithi Rao has written several short stories for young people. She also writes for television and films. Her first book was *Shakuntala and Other Stories from Ancient India*.

Comprehension

Quick Recap

A. Answer the questions in a few lines.

1. How did Gopala and his friends go to school?
2. Why were the children excited?
3. How did the boys from Stoney Hill High School behave with Gopala and his friends? Why?
4. Who was Mr Kirtan? How did he try to handle the difficult situation in his shop?
5. Why did Gopala hit Sunil? What did Mani Sir think of the fight?

6. According to Mani Sir, why was Gopala suspended?
7. Describe the place where Mani Sir found Gopala. The description uses two figures of speech. Explain them in your own words.

B. Answer the questions with reference to context.

1. *Children are naughty. Talkative. Boisterous. These children were none of those.*
   a. Who were 'these children'? Where were they at the time?
   b. Who had these thoughts about the children? What had he just said to the children?
   c. How were 'these children' different from the others?
2. *Sunil turned away dismissively and said, 'Mr Kirtan, I'll take this beyblade and those computer games.'*
   a. Who was Sunil? Why did he say these words?
   b. What were Sunil and his friends doing?
   c. What did Sunil eventually threaten to do if he did not get what he wanted?
3. *'There is no wrong or right, Sir. Only people with money and those without. My Gopala is finished.'*
   a. Who were these words spoken to? Why did Gopala's mother say these words?
   b. Why did she say that Gopala was 'finished'?
   c. What events had brought about such a change in Gopala's life?
4. *Gopala turned away. 'Neither could I,' he said, almost to himself. 'But there is something you can do,' said Mani Sir cheerfully.*
   a. What were Gopala and Mani Sir talking about in these lines?
   b. What did Gopala mean when he said 'Neither could I'?
   c. What did Gopala do next?
   d. Why do you think Mani Sir suggested that Gopala do something?

Life Skills and Values sympathy for the less privileged, teacher's role

Think and answer.

1. What are the differences between the two groups of boys in the story? Give examples to support your answer.
2. Do you think Gopala was unjustly punished? Give reasons for your answer.
3. What do you think the title of the story means?
4. What do you think of Mani Sir? Which actions of his showed that he was intelligent and sensitive?

21ST CENTURY Critical Thinking

HC Contribution in others' lives

Way with Words

WORD FAMILIES

Words formed from the same base word belong to the same word family. The words may be formed by adding or removing letters, or by adding prefixes and suffixes to the base word.

Examples: child childish childishly childlike childhood childishness

A. Create word families for the following words.

1. trouble
2. entertain
3. reason
4. silent
5. passion
6. commit

WORDS DESCRIBING CHARACTER AND PERSONALITY

People react to a situation in various ways depending on their character and personality.

Examples: Gopala was a **quiet** fellow. He did not talk much in class.
Gopala's mother was **alarmed**. She was worried that Mani Sir would scold her son.

B. Match the qualities or attitudes in column A with the actions in column B.

A	B
1. Mr Sharma is very **nervous** about travelling by air.	a. He does not like to sit still for a moment.
2. Jamshed is **boisterous**.	b. She is always the life of the party.
3. Sneha is usually very **animated**.	c. He has asked his son to accompany him on his flight to Delhi.
4. Raghu was **indifferent** to football.	d. It ran away when the children approached it with biscuits.
5. The dog was **wary** of humans.	e. He did not join the discussion on the World Cup final.

Grammar in Use

TYPES OF SENTENCES AND THEIR TRANSFORMATION

You know that sentences are of four types, based on their meaning. Look at the table on the next page, which explains these types.

Type of Sentence	Definition	Examples
Assertive	They make a statement. They can be positive or negative. These sentences end with a full stop.	Gopala was a quiet fellow. I don't know the local language.
Interrogative	They are used to ask questions. These sentences end with a question mark.	How do I explain it to these chaps? So you were thinking to buy all those toys in that pile?
Exclamatory	They are used to express strong emotions. These sentences end with an exclamation mark.	What a beautiful beyblade, with swirls of blue and yellow!
Imperative	They are used to give a command, make a request or extend an invitation.	Please tell me where he is.

A sentence can be converted from one type to another without changing its meaning.

Examples: 1. Can we ever forget the suffering of people in Hurricane Katrina?
We can never forget the suffering of people in Hurricane Katrina.
(interrogative to assertive and vice versa)

2. How tasty that dish is!
That dish is very tasty. **(exclamatory to assertive and vice versa)**

3. Shut the door.
The door should be shut. **(imperative to assertive and vice versa)**

We can also change positive sentences to negative and vice versa in these ways:

1. Using antonyms of some words in the sentence.
Example: The violence was **wrong**.
The violence was **not right**.

2. Converting a sentence into a negative interrogative sentence.
Example: Nobody **noticed** Mani Sir enter the store.
Didn't anybody notice Mani Sir enter the store?

3. Replacing the word *only* with *none but*.
Example: **Only** Mani Sir prevented a full-fledged fight.
None but Mani Sir prevented a full-fledged fight.

A. Rewrite the sentences according to the instructions given.

1. Was it such a difficult problem to solve? (change to assertive)
2. Justice delayed is justice denied. (change to interrogative)
3. The plan is perfect. (change to exclamatory)
4. What a wonderful stroke of luck! (change to assertive)
5. The captain should be asked to come to the ship's deck immediately. (change to imperative)
6. How Ananta and his friends were looking forward to buying the beyblade that day! (change to assertive)

B. Convert the sentences from positive to negative and vice versa without changing their meaning.

1. She did not ask for the project.
2. Tapan is always kind to the stray animals in his area.
3. My father forgot to post the important parcel.
4. There is no use going to the mall now.
5. This is not the way to the railway station.
6. Roohi wants to participate in the concert.

Conditional Sentences

Sentences beginning with *if* express a condition based on which the rest of the action in the sentence follows. Such sentences are described as **conditionals** or **conditional sentences**.

They are made up of two clauses: the subordinate clause — that contains the condition — and the main clause that contains the outcome if the condition is fulfilled.

Example: If you sell that beyblade to those villagers (subordinate clause with 'if' condition), I'll make sure my friends and I never buy stuff from you (main clause with the outcome).

Conditional sentences are of three types.

1. In first conditional sentences, the possibility of the condition being fulfilled is very high. First conditionals have the structure: *if* + simple present (condition), *will* + verb (result).

Example: If Gopala studies every day, he will get good marks in the test.

2. In second conditional sentences, it is possible to fulfil the condition, but it is unlikely to happen. Second conditionals have the structure: *if* + simple past (condition), *would* + verb (result).

Example: If I were richer, I would rule the world.

3. In third conditional sentences, there is no possibility of the condition being fulfilled as it refers to the past. Third conditionals have the structure: *if* + past perfect (condition), *would have* + past participle (result).

Example: If the school hadn't suspended him, the other boy's parents would have gone to the police and made things worse for Gopala.

C. Join each pair of sentences to form conditional sentences.

1. I did not know he was a criminal. I voted for him.
2. We might have met up. We did not start together.
3. He would be happy. His sister did not win the award.
4. I shall be too nervous to speak. I will meet the Chief Minister.
5. The land might have been saved. The dam should not have been built.
6. I would share Megha's address with you. I had her address.

Forming Abstract Nouns from Verbs and Adjectives

D. Complete the sentences with abstract nouns formed from the following verbs or adjectives.

please   know   clear   high   uneasy   deceive

1. Since the project was not well planned, there was no ____________ on what we had to do.
2. Looking down from a great ____________ atop the mountain, Darshan felt afraid.
3. Mala felt a sense of ____________ as she entered the abandoned house.
4. The lies and ____________ of the village headman will lead to his defeat in the coming elections.
5. ____________ is not always found in books.
6. It was my ____________ to show you around the city.

Study Skills

Use Your Dictionary

Consult an advanced dictionary to complete the table for the following words. One is done for you.

Word	*fruit*	*settlement*	*fork*	*stepped*
Parts of speech	noun, verb			
Other forms	fruits (plural), fruited (past tense)			
Meanings	n. the sweet and fleshy part of a tree that has a seed and is eaten as food v. produce fruit			
Sentences	n. Eating fruits for breakfast is healthy. v. This mango tree fruits once a year.			
Word collocations	in fruit, bear fruit			
Idiomatic expressions	bear fruit, forbidden fruit, fruit of the vine (grapes)			

Listening and Speaking

Listen to an interview of a young boy who has been forced to leave his home because of an industrial project in his area. Then, enact an interview between a journalist from a news channel and Gopala, where he is asked about being displaced from his home.

You can use the following phrases to introduce the questions:

- I would like to ask ...
- Can you share with us your experience of ...
- I am interested in knowing about...
- Can you tell us more about ...

Pen it Down

Write a formal letter to the Principal of your school, drawing his/her attention to an injustice you have faced on campus, such as bullying or being wrongfully accused of something you did not do. Explain the situation clearly and seek a solution.

You can use the following points in your letter:

- one student's word against the opinion of many
- the guilty not being punished
- how other students might face the same situation

HC Observing the desire for justice and transparency

Self Assessment

Now I can

- learn about the circumstances of people who lose their homes.
- understand the role a sympathetic teacher can play in the lives of children.
- practise word families, revise types of sentences and their transformation, use conditional sentences and form abstract nouns.
- enact an interview and write a formal letter.

Read More

Polka Dotted Party: This story, from the book *Growing Up in Pandupur*, is about Raghav, who gets to know and understand the less privileged children in his small town when he falls ill just before his birthday.

Malgudi Days: This collection of stories by R. K. Narayan narrates the stories of the ordinary people who live in the fictional town of Malgudi, including an astrologer who meets his long-forgotten rival and a boy who failed his intermediate exams ten times.

3

Conservation

Felling of the Banyan Tree

Dilip Chitre

Let's Get Started

The United Nations Sustainable Development Goal 15 asks us to sustainably manage forests, combat land degradation that forms deserts due to human activities, and halt biodiversity loss.

A. Look at this picture showing some women from the Chipko movement (1973), spearheaded by Gaura Devi. What do you think the women are doing here? Say two lines about the picture in class.

B. Have you heard of the term 'eco-warrior'? Look at these images with suggestions on how you can be an eco-warrior. Form groups of six, with each group taking up one of the points. Write a few sentences on the chosen idea and then share your thoughts with the other groups.

Eco-Warrior Starter Kit

local produce

awareness generation

a cycle instead of a car

eco-tourism

eco-friendly clothing

reusable cups and plates

HC **Active Participation:** Understanding the purpose of and interconnectedness between the plant and the human order

Reading

Do you have trees around your house? Do you feel a sense of attachment towards them? Read this poem on the sense of loss the speaker feels on the felling of a much-loved banyan tree.

Where did the tenants live?

My father told the **tenants** to leave
Who lived on the houses surrounding our house on the hill
One by one the structures were demolished
Only our own house remained and the trees
Trees are **sacred** my grandmother used to say
Felling them is a crime but he **massacred** them all
The sheoga, the oudumber, the neem were all cut down
But the huge banyan tree stood like a problem
Whose roots lay deeper than all our lives
My father ordered it to be removed
The banyan tree was three times as tall as our house
Its trunk had a circumference of fifty feet
Its **scraggy aerial roots** fell to the ground
From thirty feet or more so first they cut the branches
Sawing them off for seven days and the heap was huge
Insects and birds began to leave the tree
And then they came to its massive trunk
Fifty men with axes chopped and chopped
The great tree revealed its **rings** of two hundred years
We watched in terror and fascination this slaughter
As a raw mythology revealed to us its age
Soon afterwards we left Baroda for Bombay
Where there are no trees except the one
Which grows and **seethes** in one's dreams, its aerial roots
Looking for the ground to strike.

Wordwise

The word 'banyan' comes from the Sanskrit word, 'vanija' meaning 'merchant'. Early foreign traders mention Indian merchants doing business under this tree. The word has since passed into English to refer to the tree itself.

tenants: people who pay rent to live in a room or house

sacred: holy

felling: chopping

massacred: killed violently

scraggy: thin and rough

aerial roots: roots that grow above the ground

rings: (here) the concentric rings in the cross section of a tree trunk, which indicate the tree's age

seethes: moves around quickly and violently

About the poet

Dilip Chitre (1938–2009) was one of the most important poets in post-Independence India. He wrote in Marathi and English. Some of his best-known works include a translation of the poems of the Marathi Bhakti poet, Sant Tukaram, and the poetry collections, *Shesha* and *As Is Where Is*. He received the Sahitya Akademi Award for his collection of Marathi poems in 1994.

Comprehension

Quick Recap

A. Answer the questions with reference to context.

1. *Trees are sacred my grandmother used to say/Felling them is a crime but he massacred them all*
   a. Who is the speaker in these lines? Who is the person referred to as 'he'?
   b. Name the trees that were cut down. Why are 'his' actions referred to as a 'crime'?
   c. What else had this person done?
   d. What do you conclude about the speaker's feelings from the lines?
2. *My father ordered it to be removed*
   a. What does the word 'it' refer to? Describe it in your own words.
   b. What is 'it' compared to? Explain the figure of speech used here in your own words.
   c. How was it removed?
   d. What happened when it began to be 'removed'?
3. *We watched in terror and fascination this slaughter*
   a. Why did the speaker experience the opposing feelings of 'terror' and 'fascination'?
   b. What did the 'slaughter' reveal?
   c. Why is the slaughter referred to as 'raw mythology'?
   d. Which other word in the poem, apart from 'mythology', suggests the special nature of the banyan tree?
4. *Where there are no trees except the one/Which grows and seethes in one's dreams*
   a. Which place does the word 'where' refer to? Where did the speaker's family originally stay?
   b. Which tree does the speaker refer to in the given lines? Is it a real tree?
   c. What does the tree do? Explain the phrase 'grows and seethes in one's dreams'.

Life Skills and Values — love for nature, conservation

Think and answer.

1. Why do you think the speaker's father asked the tenants to leave and had all the trees cut down?
2. Why does the speaker describe the felling of the tree as an act of violence? Which words in the poem suggest so?
3. What kind of a person do you think the speaker is? How does the death of the tree become the symbol of a deeper loss for him?
4. What is the message of the poem with regard to the environment?

Way with Words

Contextual Usage

A. Complete the sentences with the correct form of the words from the poem.

1. The scientist was ________________ by his own discovery. (fascination)
2. Sidney Poitier was a ________________ as an actor in the film *To Sir, With Love.* (revealed)
3. The corporation ordered the ________________ of a heritage building. (demolished)
4. Wasting food is ________________ as people around the world die of hunger every day. (crime)
5. The bully ________________ the timid boy into doing his homework. (terror)
6. After Timothy came back from a month-long vacation, he had an impressive ________________ of hair on his face. (grows)

Words and Phrases Related to Plants

There are many idioms and phrasal verbs related to plants in English.

Examples: My **roots** are in Gujarat, but I have lived in Mumbai all my life. (place of origin)
His business started doing well after he **branched out** in a new direction. (expand)

B. Write the meanings of the underlined words and phrases related to plants in these sentences.

1. Shweta decided to <u>take a leaf out of</u> her hard-working friend's <u>book</u> and study for an hour more every day.
2. The NGO works with people <u>at the grassroots</u>.
3. The journalist's confidence <u>shrivelled up</u> after a rebuke from his superior.
4. The young cricketer is a <u>budding</u> genius. In another five years, he will be the captain of the national team.
5. The people's anger <u>stems</u> from their belief that their king does not care for them.
6. If you try to persuade a miser to lend you money, you would be <u>barking up the wrong tree</u>.

Grammar in Use

Reflexive Pronouns

Read these sentences.

Be careful with the saw. You might hurt **yourself**.
The tenants decided among **themselves** that they would not listen to the cruel landlord.

In these sentences, the pronouns **yourself** and **themselves** refer to the subjects of the sentences. Such pronouns are called **reflexive pronouns**.

They include **myself**, **yourself**, **himself**, **herself**, **ourselves**, **yourselves**, **themselves** and **itself**.

A. Complete the sentences with reflexive pronouns.

1. Don't be so hard on ________________.
2. Joyee is fifteen. She is old enough to go to school by ________________ now.
3. The robbers divided up the loot between ________________.
4. Sam looked at ________________ in the mirror for the first time in two days and was surprised at his rough appearance.
5. The plan ________________ was not bad, but it was poorly carried out.
6. We painted the house ________________, without any help.
7. I have set ________________ a target of completing two chapters in a day.

Subject–Verb Agreement

Look at this sentence.

The banyan tree was three times as tall as our house.

In this sentence, the subject **the banyan tree** is singular, so it is followed by the singular verb 'was'.

Now, look at this sentence.

Trees are sacred, my grandmother used to say.

The subject of the sentence is the noun **trees** which is plural, so the verb following the subject, **are** is also plural.

The verb must agree with the subject in number and person for a sentence to be grammatically correct. This is known as the **agreement of subject and verb**.

There are some basic rules of subject–verb agreement.

1. When a collective noun is considered as a single unit, it takes a singular verb.
   Example: The heap of fallen leaves **was** huge.
2. If members or units that make up the collective noun are considered as individuals, then we use a plural verb.
   Example: Some of the household staff **were** not present when the trees were being cut.
3. Two singular subjects joined by *or*, *either ... or* or *neither ... nor* take a singular verb.
   Example: Neither the sheoga nor the neem **was** spared of the felling.

4. However, when *either ... or* or *neither ... nor* are used with two subjects, one of whom is different from the other in number or person, the verb agrees with the subject nearest to it.

   Examples: Either the father or the fifty men **were** responsible for the felling of the tree.
   Neither the men nor the father **feels** guilty about felling the tree.

5. When words like *each* or *every* are used before a noun, the verb is singular.

   Example: Each tree **was** cut down mercilessly.

6. We use a plural verb with quantifiers such as *both*, *few* and *many*, while *much* always takes a singular verb.

   Examples: Both the neem and the banyan **were** felled.
   Few people **are** conscious about the impact of cutting trees on the environment.
   Much of the roots of the tree **was** exposed.

B. Identify the errors in these sentences and rewrite them correctly.

1. Many people is laughing at his antics on social media now.
2. Either the train is late or the timetable have changed.
3. The jury was divided in its final verdict.
4. The army of ants were carrying off the fallen cubes of sugar.
5. Both Joe and his father is frontline Covid warriors.
6. Both Lovlina Borgohain and P. V. Sindhu is Olympic bronze medallists.

Study Skills

Pronounce Well

You have studied that words can be divided into syllables. A syllable is a unit of sound or pronunciation. A word can be made up of one, two, three or more syllables.

Examples: hill (one syllable)
felling: fell/ing (two syllables)
afterwards: af/ter/wards (three syllables)

The following words are divided into their constituent syllables. Choose the correct option. (Remember that each syllable has only one distinct vowel sound.)

1. **never:**	a. nev/er	b. never	
2. **hundred:**	a. hun/dred	b. hu/n/dred	
3. **happened:**	a. hap/pened	b. hap/pen/ed	
4. **climate:**	a. cli/mate	b. cl/i/mate	
5. **George:**	a. George	b. Geor/ge	c. Ge/or/ge
6. **moisture:**	a. moi/st/ure	b. mois/ture	c. mo/is/ture
7. **commentator:**	a. commen/tator	b. com/men/ta/tor	c. com/men/tator
8. **appreciation:**	a. ap/pre/cia/tion	b. ap/pre/ci/a/tion	c. app/re/ci/ation

Listening and Speaking

Listen to a group discussion on people being indifferent about saving the environment. Then, have a group discussion on the topic 'How does felling trees harm the environment?'

Keep the following points in mind for the group discussion:

- Ensure that your facts are correct before you use them to support your opinions.
- Always pay close attention to what is being said, before responding.
- Be polite when disagreeing with someone's opinions.

Pen it Down

Write a formal letter to your local municipal councillor, complaining about the indiscriminate felling of trees in your locality and the fallout of such actions.

You can include the following points in your letter:

- steps to be taken to stop the practice
- how the guilty may be caught and punished
- drive to plant new trees

Self Assessment

Now I can

- note how Nature is sacrificed for the sake of progress and development.
- practise words and phrases related to plants, use reflexive pronouns and understand the rules of subject–verb agreement.
- pronounce stressed and unstressed syllables correctly, have a group discussion on a given topic and write a formal letter.

Read More

On Killing a Tree: Through its graphic description of the chopping of a tree, this poem by Gieve Patel draws attention to the destructive ways of human beings who have caused lasting harm to ever-resilient Nature.

Tree at my Window: This poem by Robert Frost describes the close relationship the speaker feels with a tree outside his window, as it watches him go through good and bad times.

Horror Fiction

4

The Monkey's Paw

W. W. Jacobs

Let's Get Started

Do you like listening to scary stories? What emotions do you go through then? Read these examples of short scary stories. Then work in groups of five and write a scary story that is not more than three sentences long.

- Someone whispered in my ears. When I turned around, nobody was there.
- I saw someone move behind the curtains. I knew I was the only person living in the house.
- Mr Jenkins still visits his granddaughter from time to time. Mr Jenkins has been dead for three years.
- I looked under the bed. The monster looked back at me.

HC **Active Participation:** Exploring maintenance of balance in orders

Reading

Have you ever wished for something quite deeply? Did you come to regret it when the wish came true? Read this story to find out what happens to a family when their wishes start coming true.

'Be careful what you wish for, you may receive it.'– Anonymous

Outside, the night was cold and wet, but in the living room the curtains were closed and the fire burned brightly. Father and son were playing chess.

'Listen to the wind,' said Mr White. 'I should hardly think that he'll come tonight.'

'There he is,' said Herbert White as the gate banged shut loudly and heavy footsteps came towards the door.

Why did the family not expect a visitor that night?

The old man rose quickly and opened the door to a tall, heavy built, strong man.

'**Sergeant-Major** Morris,' he said, introducing him to his wife and his son, Herbert.

The Sergeant-Major shook hands and, taking the offered seat by the fire, began to talk. The little family circle listened with growing interest to this visitor from **distant parts**, as he spoke of wild scenes and brave acts; of wars and strange people.

'What was that that you started telling me the other day about a monkey's paw or something, Morris?'

'Well, it's just a bit of what you might call magic, perhaps,' said the Sergeant-Major.

His three listeners leaned forward excitedly.

'To look at it,' said the Sergeant-Major, 'it's just an ordinary little paw, dried to a mummy.'

He took something out of his pocket and held it out for them. Mrs White drew back with a look of disgust, but her son, taking it, examined it curiously.

'It had a spell put on it by an old fakir,' said the Sergeant-Major, 'a very holy man. He wanted to show that fate ruled people's lives, and that those who tried to change it would be sorry. He put a spell on it so that three different men could each have three wishes from it.'

The way he told the story showed that he truly believed it. His voice was so serious that the group fell quiet.

The Sergeant-Major continued, 'I did have some idea of selling it, but I don't think I will. It has caused me enough trouble already.'

'If you don't want it Morris,' said Mr White, 'give it to me.'

'If you keep it, don't hold me responsible for what happens,' said his friend with stubborn determination.

The other shook his head and examined his new possession closely. 'So, how do you do it?' he asked.

Sergeant-Major: an officer in the British army responsible for organizing the affairs of a regiment

distant parts: faraway places

Did You Know? G.K.

A mummy is a person or an animal whose body has been preserved after death. The mummy of King Tutankhamun, which is more than 3,000 years old, is possibly the most well-known specimen ever discovered.

Wordwise

'Fakir' is an Arabic term for a sage or a monk who has mystical powers. A fakir is a spiritual person who has given up all material wealth.

'Hold it up in your right hand, and state your wish out loud so that you can be heard,' said the Sergeant-Major. 'But I warn you of what might happen. If you must wish, wish for something sensible.'

Mr White dropped it back in his pocket. Dinner began and the **talisman** was partly forgotten.

'I wonder if the tale of the monkey's paw is true,' said Herbert, after their guest had left. 'If it is, we're going to be rich, and famous, and happy.'

Mr White took the paw from his pocket and eyed it doubtfully. 'I don't know what to wish for, and that's a fact,' he said slowly. 'It seems to me I've got all I want.'

'If you only paid off the house, you'd be quite happy, wouldn't you!' said Herbert, with his hand on his shoulder. 'Well, wish for two hundred pounds, then; that'll just do it.'

His father, smiling and embarrassed for his foolishness in believing the soldier's story, held up the talisman.

'I wish for two hundred pounds,' said the old man clearly.

There was a sudden frightened cry from him. His wife and son came running.

'It moved,' he cried, with a look of horror at the object as it lay on the floor where he had thrown it. 'As I wished, it twisted in my hand like a snake.'

'Well, I don't see the money,' said his son, as he picked the paw up and placed it on the table, 'and I bet I never shall.'

'It must have been your imagination,' said Mrs White, regarding him worriedly.

He shook his head. 'Never mind, though; there's no harm done, but it gave me a shock all the same.'

Outside, the wind was higher than ever, and an unusual and **depressing** silence settled on all three until the family got up to go to bed.

talisman: an object thought to have magic powers

depressing: gloomy

fashion: (here) manner

Why did Herbert want Mr White to wish for two hundred pounds?

The next morning, Herbert had left for work, and the dirty, dried-up little paw was thrown on the cabinet with a carelessness which indicated no great belief in what good it could do.

'The idea of our listening to such nonsense! How could wishes be granted in these days? And if they could, how could two hundred pounds hurt you?' said Mrs White.

'Morris said the things happened so naturally,' said Mr White, 'that you might if you so wished not see the relationship. I had just — What's the matter?'

His wife made no reply. She was watching the mysterious movements of a well-dressed man outside, who, looking in an undecided **fashion** at the house, appeared to be trying to make up his mind to enter. Three times he stopped briefly at the gate, and then walked on again. The fourth time he stood with his hand upon it, and then with sudden **firmness** of mind pushed it open and walked up the path. Mrs White went to the door.

Where had the stranger come from?

She brought in the stranger, who seemed a little uncomfortable, into the room.

firmness: (here) strength; determination

firm: (here) a company or an organisation

'I — was asked to call,' he said at last, 'I come from "Maw and Meggins."'

The old lady jumped suddenly, alarmed. 'Is anything the matter?' she asked breathlessly. 'Has anything happened to Herbert? What is it? What is it?'

Her husband spoke before the man could answer. 'There, there,' he said hurriedly. 'Sit down, and don't jump to a conclusion. You've not brought bad news, I'm sure sir,' and eyed the other, expecting that it was bad news but hoping he was wrong.

'I'm sorry—' began the visitor.

'Is he hurt?' demanded the mother wildly.

The visitor lowered and raised his head once in agreement. 'Badly hurt,' he said quietly, 'but he is not in any pain.'

'Oh thank God!' said the old woman, pressing her hands together tightly. 'Thank God for that! Thank—'

She broke off as the tragic meaning of the part about him not being in pain came to her. The man had turned his head slightly so as not to look directly at her, but she saw the awful truth in his face. She caught her breath, and turning to her husband, who did not yet understand the man's meaning, laid her shaking hand on his. There was a long silence.

'He was caught in the machinery,' said the visitor at length in a low voice. 'The **firm** wishes me to pass on their great sadness about your loss,' he said.

'I was to say that "Maw and Meggins" accept no responsibility,' he continued, 'and they don't have a legal requirement to make a payment for your loss, but in view of your son's services they wish to present you with a certain sum.'

Mr White dropped his wife's hand, and rising to his feet, stared with a look of horror at his visitor. His dry lips shaped the words, 'How much?'

'Two hundred pounds,' was the answer.

Without hearing his wife's scream, the old man smiled weakly and fell, a senseless mass, to the floor.

In the huge **cemetery** some two miles away, the old people buried their dead, and came back to the house which was now full of shadows and silence. It was all over so quickly that at first they could hardly realize it, and remained in a state of waiting for something else to happen to lighten this load, too heavy for old hearts to bear.

But the days passed, and they realized that they had to accept the situation. Sometimes they hardly said a word to each other, for now they had nothing to talk about, and their days were long.

It was about a week later that the old man, waking suddenly in the night, heard the sound of his wife crying quietly at the window.

'Come back,' he said tenderly. 'You will be cold.'

'It is colder for my son,' said the old woman, who began crying again.

But then, she exclaimed wildly, 'The paw! The monkey's paw!'

He started up in alarm. 'What's the matter?'

She almost fell as she came hurried across the room towards him. 'I want it,' she said quietly. 'You've not destroyed it?'

'It's in the living room, on the shelf above the fire place,' he replied. 'Why?'

She cried and laughed together, and bending over, kissed his cheek.

'I only just thought of it,' she said. 'Why didn't I think of it before? Why didn't you think of it?'

'Think of what?' he questioned.

'The other two wishes,' she replied quickly. 'We've only had one.'

'Was not that enough?' he demanded angrily.

'No,' she cried excitedly. 'We'll have one more. Go down and get it quickly, and wish our boy alive again.'

cemetery: graveyard

coincidence: when two or more similar or related events occur at the same time by chance and without any planning

What did the mother want the father to wish for?

Mr White struck a match and lit a candle. 'Get back to bed,' he said, his voice shaking. 'You don't know what you are saying.'

'We had the first wish granted,' said the old woman, desperately, 'why not the second?'

'A c-c-**coincidence**,' said the old man.

'Go get it and wish,' cried his wife, shaking with excitement.

The old man turned and looked at her. 'He has been dead ten days!'

'Bring him back,' cried the old woman, and pulled him towards the door. 'Do you think I fear my child?'

He went down in the darkness. The talisman was in its place on the shelf.

Even his wife's face seemed changed as he entered the room. It was white and **expectant**, and to his fear, it seemed to have an unnatural look upon it. He was afraid of her.

'Wish!' she cried in a strong voice.

He raised his hand. 'I wish my son alive again.'

The talisman fell to the floor, and he looked at it fearfully. Then he sank into a chair and the old woman, with burning eyes, walked to the window and opened the curtains.

When the candle, which had almost burned to the bottom, finally went out, the old man, with an **unspeakable** sense of relief at the failure of the talisman, went slowly back to his bed. A minute afterward, the old woman came silently and lay without movement beside him.

The darkness was depressing, and after lying for some time, building up his courage, the husband took the box of matches, and lighting one, went downstairs for another candle. At the foot of the stairs the match went out, and at the same moment, a knock sounded on the front door. The matches fell from Mr White's hand. He stood **motionless**, not even breathing, until the knock was repeated. Then he turned and ran quickly back to his room, and closed the door behind him. A third knock sounded through the house.

'It's Herbert!' Mrs White screamed. 'It's Herbert!'

She ran to the door, but her husband was there before her, and catching her by the arm, held her tightly. 'What are you going to do?' he asked in a low, scared voice.

'It's my boy; it's Herbert!' she cried. 'I forgot it was two miles away. I must open the door.'

'For God's sake, don't let it in,' cried the old man, shaking with fear.

'You're afraid of your own son,' she cried struggling. 'Let me go. I'm coming, Herbert, I'm coming.'

There was another knock, and another. The old woman broke free with a sudden pull and ran from the room. Her husband

expectant: hoping for something

unspeakable: that cannot be described in words

motionless: not moving at all

Why was Mr White not letting go of Mrs White?

followed to the top of the stairs, and called after her as she hurried down. He was on his hands and knees, feeling around wildly on the floor in search of the paw. If only he could find it before the thing outside got in. The knocks came very quickly now echoing through the house, and he heard the noise of his wife moving a chair and putting it down against the door, to reach the top lock. She began to open the lock, and at the same moment he found the monkey's paw, and **frantically** breathed his third and last wish.

frantically: in a wild and uncontrolled way

deserted: with no people in it

The knocking stopped suddenly. He heard the door open and then, a long loud cry of disappointment and pain from his wife gave him the courage to run down to her side, and then to the gate. The streetlight opposite shone on a quiet and **deserted** road.

About the author

William Wymark Jacobs (1863–1943) was an English author who wrote short stories and novels. He is most well-known for his humorous comedies involving characters from rural England. He also wrote a few horror stories, the most well-known of which is 'The Monkey's Paw'.

Comprehension

Quick Recap

A. Complete the table with suitable causes and effects.

Cause	Effect
1.	a. The family fell quiet while listening to Sergeant-Major Morris speaking about the monkey's paw.
2. Herbert reminded Mr White about the mortgage on the house.	b.
3.	c. The monkey's paw twisted like a snake in Mr White's hand.
4.	d. Someone from 'Maw and Meggins' came to see Mr and Mrs White.
5. Mrs White insisted that her husband wish for their son to be alive again.	e.
6.	f. The knocking on the door stopped suddenly.

B. Answer the questions with reference to context.

1. *He took something out of his pocket and held it out for them.*
   a. Who took something out from his pocket? What was it?

b. Who did 'them' refer to? What were their reactions to the object?

c. What was the tale associated with the object?

2. *'Never mind, though; there's no harm done, but it gave me a shock all the same.'*

a. Who said these words and to whom?

b. What had given him a shock?

c. Do you think there really was 'no harm done'? Give reasons for your answer.

3. *'He was caught in the machinery,' said the visitor at length in a low voice.*

a. Who did 'he' refer to? What had happened to him?

b. What compensation was offered to 'his' parents? Why was the amount significant?

c. Explain the symbolism in the phrase 'caught in the machinery'.

4. *'For God's sake, don't let it in,'*

a. Who said these words and to whom?

b. What does the word 'it' refer to?

c. Why was the speaker afraid of letting 'it' in? Why was the listener trying to let 'it' in?

Life Skills and Values consequences of greed, handling grief

Think and answer.

1. How did the fakir's lesson affect the White family? Do you think Mr White was responsible for the tragedy because of his greed?
2. Mr and Mrs White's son had died tragically. Do you think their efforts to bring Herbert back from the dead stemmed from the intense grief they felt? Explain your answer.
3. *Be careful what you wish for, you may receive it* – How does the story illustrate this saying? Do you agree that we should be careful while wishing for something? Why/Why not?

21ST CENTURY Critical Thinking

Way with Words

Words Related to Horror

A. Fill in the blanks with suitable words from the box.

phantom	bloodcurdling	petrified	haunted	eerie	cemetery

1. We were nervous about staying in the bungalow as it was rumoured to be ________.
2. From the distance we could hear a ________ scream.
3. It was pitch black outside, and an ________ silence enveloped the street.
4. When Ratul saw a tall figure lurking behind him, he was ________.

5. Every night, the villagers heard strange sounds coming from the ______________.
6. The old lady screamed in the middle of the night, claiming to have seen a ______________.

Idioms Related to Fear

In the story, you have come across the idiom **jump to a conclusion**. It means to make a decision about somebody/something too quickly, before knowing or having thought about all the facts. Mrs White had already imagined the worst the moment the visitor told her that he had come from her son's workplace.

B. Match these idioms related to fear in Column A with their meanings in Column B.

Idiom	Meaning
1. jump out of your skin •	• a. a sudden feeling of fear or excitement
2. make one's blood run cold •	• b. not able to move, because of fright or surprise
3. break out in a cold sweat •	• c. move violently because of a sudden shock
4. be rooted to the spot •	• d. make someone very frightened or fill them with horror
5. heart misses a beat •	• e. disappear suddenly in a mysterious way
6. vanish into thin air •	• f. be affected by a sudden unpleasant sweaty feeling

Grammar in Use

Modals

You have studied modal verbs and their functions in earlier classes. These verbs behave differently from ordinary verbs in the following ways:

- They do not change their form depending on the number or the person. So, we do not add 's' in the third person singular form of the verbs.
  Example: Well, it's just a bit of what you **might** call magic, perhaps.
- Modal verbs have no infinitive or '-ing' form.
- They can be used to form questions. **Example:** **May** I see the monkey's paw?
- Unlike other verbs, they take their negative forms without using 'do'/'did'.
  Example: You **must not** let it in. (Other verbs: Sergeant-Major Morris **did not want** to sell the monkey's paw.)

You know that modal verbs can be used to express a variety of meanings, such as possibility, permission and suggestion.

These are the commonly used modal verbs.

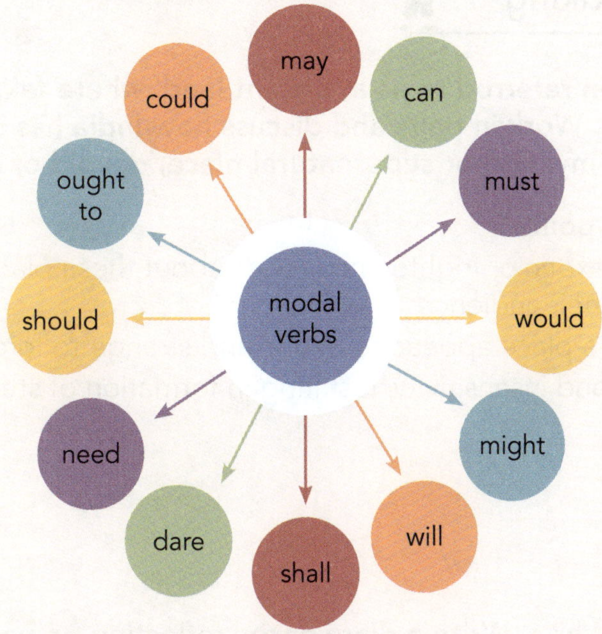

Complete the sentences with the correct modal verb, according to the instructions given. One is done for you.

1. *The meeting* *__must__* *be over by now. (certainty)*
2. ________________ I have another pastry? (request)
3. She ________________ practise harder if she wants to be selected for the basketball team. (necessity)
4. You ________________ always speak kindly to the poor lady. (advice)
5. She ________________ miss the train to London if she does not leave now. (possibility)
6. You ________________ leave right away if you like. (permission)
7. You ________________ take up swimming this summer. (suggestion)
8. Tanaya ________________ dance very well, but she is shy about performing in public. (ability)
9. I ________________ never break my promise. (resolve)

Study Skills

Spell Check

The English language is not phonetic. This means that words are often not pronounced the way they are spelt. One example of this rule are words with silent letters. **Examples:** s**c**ene, dou**b**tfully

Underline the words in the paragraph that have silent letters. Circle the letters that are silent. Some words have more than one silent letter.

A handsome and honest knight hauled Selima out and gave her a prettily designed handkerchief to sneeze into. Her master feared she might have asthma or pneumonia. But Selima recovered, and on a Wednesday, he threw a party in his castle. There were sandwiches for the guests. Selima, wearing her favourite cologne and tail erect, padded down the aisle. Long may her reign continue!

Listening and Speaking

In the story, India has been referred to as a 'distant land' where fakirs cast spells to create frightening magic objects. Work in pairs and discuss how India has often been stereotyped in the western world as a mystical or supernatural place, devoid of rational thought.

21st Century Communication

You may talk about these points:

- travellers returning with exotic or frightening stories about these places, often exaggerating with the aim to impress their audience
- the culture and rituals of a place appearing exotic and strange to foreigners
- prior lack of knowledge and insensitivity, resulting in formation of stereotypical opinions

Pen it Down

Imagine that you are Mr White. Write a diary entry, reflecting on your decision of interfering with fate and the horrors that befell your family, as a result.

21st Century Creativity

You may include these points:

- how you felt at first about believing the story about the monkey's paw
- what your first wish was and how you felt when you made the wish
- the sequence of events after the first wish
- your feelings of regret and guilt

Self Assessment

Now I can

- read and understand a horror story about how people should be careful about what they wish for.
- use words related to horror fiction, match idioms related to fear with their meanings and practise modals.
- identify words with silent letters, have a discussion on a given topic and write a diary entry.

Read More

The Tell-Tale Heart: This short story by Edgar Allan Poe is about an unnamed narrator who tries to convince the reader of his own sanity, while simultaneously describing a murder that he himself had committed.

Coraline: This novel by Neil Gaiman is about a young girl, Coraline, who has recently moved into an old house with her parents. The story describes how she must save herself and her parents from the resident evil forces that threaten them.

5 The Road Not Taken

Robert Frost

Let's Get Started

A. In life we are often met with choices which put us in conflict with others. How do you think these conflicts can be resolved reasonably?

Now, do these two activities.

Work in pairs – and stand in two lines facing each other from opposite ends of the classroom. Now walk towards each other in the same line, till both of you are face to face. Now without using words and using only gestures, resolve who will cross over first and reach the other side. There should be no display of force or rough behaviour. How long did it take you to convince or be convinced? Why?

Now play the same game again, but this time the only condition is that the person who reaches the opposite side first is the winner. Now approach your partner from the opposite side and see how long it takes. Does it take longer? Why or why not?

What do these two activities tell us about conflict resolution? Discuss in class.

B. Imagine that there is an emergency situation, and everyone must evacuate the house within minutes. Which three items from your room will you take with you and why? Share your answers with the class.

HC **Learning and Awareness:** Recognising how happiness is linked with understanding the self

Reading

Have you ever had to choose between two options that looked equally promising? There will be many occasions in your life when you will be at a crossroads and will have to choose a path.

Read this allegorical poem about a traveller who stands at a crossroads in a forest and has to make a choice.

Two roads **diverged** in a yellow wood,
And sorry I could not travel both
And be one traveller, long I stood
And looked down one as far as I could[1]
To where it bent in the **undergrowth**;

Then took the other, as just as **fair**,
And having perhaps the better **claim**,
Because it was grassy and wanted **wear**;
Though as for that the passing there
Had worn them really about the same,

And both that morning equally lay
In leaves no step had **trodden** black.
Oh, I kept the first for another day!
Yet knowing how way leads on to way,
I doubted if I should ever come back.

I shall be telling this with a sigh
Somewhere ages and ages **hence**:
Two roads diverged in a wood, and I—
I took the one less travelled by,
And that has made all the difference.

Literary term

1. This is an example of a **run-on line**. The sentences are carried over to the next line to resemble everyday speech.

How were the two roads similar?

diverged: branched off

undergrowth: small trees and plants growing under larger trees

fair: (here) promising

claim: basis for an action

wear: (here) use

trodden: walked

hence: from this time

About the poet

Robert Frost (1874–1963) was an American poet who received the Pulitzer Prize in Poetry four times. His poems often depict American rural life in the early twentieth century. Some of his best-known poems are 'Stopping by Woods on a Snowy Evening' and 'Mending Wall'.

Comprehension

Quick Recap

A. Answer the questions in a few lines.

1. Why do you think the speaker used the adjective 'yellow' to describe the wood?
2. What was the speaker's first reaction to not being able to travel both the roads?
3. How far did the speaker try to see down the first road?
4. What did the speaker decide about the first road? Why?

B. Answer the questions with reference to context.

1. *Then took the other, as just as fair,/And having perhaps the better claim*
   a. What is being referred to as 'the other'?
   b. What did the speaker mean by the phrase 'better claim'? Why did it have a better claim?
   c. Even though the 'other' had the better claim, how was it similar to another path?
2. *And both that morning equally lay/In leaves no step had trodden black.*
   a. What do the phrases 'lay in leaves' and 'trodden black' mean?
   b. What did the speaker ultimately decide to do?
   c. What did he say about his choice?
3. *I took the one less travelled by,/And that has made all the difference.*
   a. What did the speaker imagine himself saying about his choice in the future?
   b. What does the phrase 'one less travelled by' mean? Explain the last line of the poem.
   c. Why would the speaker 'sigh' while saying these lines?

Life Skills and Values — making choices

Think and answer.

1. This poem is an allegory about the choices we make. What do the two roads in the poem stand for? How can we interpret the speaker's doubts about which road to take? (21st Century: Critical Thinking)
2. Explain, in your own words, the significance of the title of the poem.
3. What can you conclude about the speaker from the choice he makes?

HC Understanding of the self, existence and universal human behaviour

Way with Words

Words with Multiple Meanings

The poet uses several words whose meanings in the poem are different from the sense in which they are usually used.

Example: In the line, 'To where it bent in the undergrowth', the word **bent** is used in the sense of 'turned'. The more common usage of the word is in the sense of 'curved'. (*He* ***bent*** *the copper wire into the shape of a rectangle.*)

A. Complete the sentences using words from the poem. The words are used in a different sense from that in the poem.

1. The prince wanted to know who the ______________ maiden, whom he had seen in the forest, was.

2. I can ________________ the money I paid at the hospital from my insurance provider.
3. Reena ________________ puzzled when the detective asked her about the missing documents.
4. The ________________ of the old year always made Maya sad.
5. Rajiv's first year of work was a whirlwind of ________________, as he visited ten countries.
6. It was a ________________ day when America dropped the atomic bomb on Japan.

Idioms and Phrases About Choice

B. Write the meanings of these phrases and idioms about choice and use them in sentences of your own.

1. on the horns of a dilemma
2. to be in a Catch-22 situation
3. fait accompli
4. Hobson's choice

Grammar in Use

Adverbs

You know that an adverb is a word that modifies a verb, an adjective or another adverb. They are of different types.

Adverbs of manner describe how an action took place.

Example: And both that morning **equally** lay.
Here, the adverb **equally** describes *how* the roads lay in the morning.

Adverbs of place describe where something happened.

Example: And looked **down** as far as I could.
Here, the adverb **down** tells us *where* the person looked.

Adverbs of time tell us when the action took place.

Example: The CEO is flying to Hong Kong **tomorrow** to attend an important meeting.
Here, the adverb **tomorrow** tells us *when* the CEO is flying to Hong Kong.

Adverbs of frequency describe how often something happened.

Example: The poet **occasionally** took long walks in the woods near his house.
Here, the adverb **occasionally** tells us *how often* the poet took long walks.

Adverbs of degree describe the intensity or degree of an action.

Example: It is **extremely** important for young people to focus on their careers.
Here, the adverb **extremely** tells us the *degree* of importance young people should give to their careers.

A. Rewrite the sentences according to the given instructions.

1. The ballerina danced *with a lot of grace.* (replace the words in italics with an adverb of manner)
2. Nowadays, we don't go to the park *too many times.* (replace the words in italics with an adverb of frequency)
3. She ________________ sleeps late. (use an adverb of frequency)
4. The athlete ran ________________ fast and beat the others to the finishing line. (use an adverb of degree)
5. The Earth will ________________ run out of resources if we don't make an effort to protect it. (use an adverb of time)
6. Preeti searched *in every place*, but could not find her purse. (replace the words in italics with an adverb of place)

Phrases and Clauses

A **phrase** is a group of words which conveys a meaning but does not make complete sense by itself. A **clause**, unlike a phrase, is a group of words which contains a subject and a finite verb.

A phrase can be converted into a clause in a sentence without changing its meaning. Look at the phrases in the following sentences.

He seems **to be a traveller**.

The sudden fork in the road was totally unexpected.

In these sentences, the phrases can be rewritten as clauses.

It seems **that he is a traveller**.

That the road would suddenly fork was totally unexpected.

B. Underline the clauses in the following sentences. Then, rewrite the sentences after replacing the clauses with phrases that mean the same.

1. I am going to have a proper meal when I reach home.
2. While he was reading a book, Robert fell asleep.
3. I hope that I will finish my paper in time.
4. Everyone knows that he is an honest man.
5. The teachers expected that his performance will improve.

Study Skills

Pronounce well

Divide these words into stressed and unstressed syllables. Then, underline the word that differs from the rest in the position of the stressed syllable. One is done for you.

	a.	b.	c.
1.	*'u/ni/form*	*'o/cean*	*ma/'te/rial*
2.	another	grandmother	delicious
3.	holiday	lukewarm	explode

4. a. bedside b. neglect c. hygiene
5. a. intention b. examine c. sensible
6. a. yellow b. knowing c. because

Listening and Speaking

Listen to a passage about a boy who makes a difficult choice and answer these questions.

1. Where did Shyam live and why was he at the station?
2. Where had he gone and why?
3. Who did Shyam speak to at the station?
4. Why did Shyam want to go to Mumbai?
5. What did he see at the station that made him want to do so?
6. Whom did he know in Mumbai? What was his profession?
7. What had this person done earlier?
8. What choice did he have to make and why?

Pen it Down

Imagine that you have joined a new school, and you are not sure which extra-curricular club you would like to join. Write an email to your cousin, explaining your dilemma, and ask for his/her suggestions to help you make a choice.

You can include the following points in your email:

- what you find interesting about each club
- which club would suit your skills the best
- how this club would help you grow as a student

Self Assessment

Now I can

- understand how our lives are shaped by the choices we make.
- learn about idioms and phrases related to choice, practise adverbs, and understand the difference between phrases and clauses.
- separate words into stressed and unstressed syllables, and write an email.

Read More

Stopping by Woods on a Snowy Evening: This poem by Robert Frost is about a man who stops to spend a few moments while passing through a forest on a winter night.

The Choice: This poem by Robert William Service talks about the various qualities that people would want if given a choice. The poet himself wants only the power of imagination and the ability to write good poetry.

6
A Tale of Two Cities

Charles Dickens

Let's Get Started

The United Nations Sustainable Development Goal 11 states that cities should provide opportunities for all, with access to basic services, such as energy, housing, transportation and healthcare.

Look at this mind map and recreate it in an A4 sheet. Work in pairs, and write five things each that you like and dislike about your city or locality. You can also use images to highlight the points.

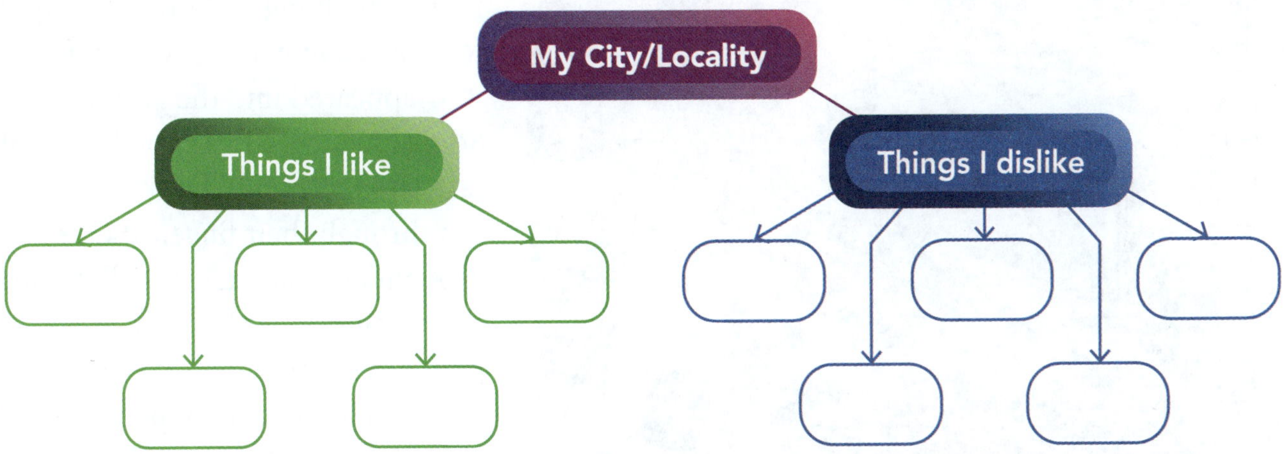

Active Participation: Participating in Society – helping in maintaining systems

Reading

***A Tale of Two Cities** is set against the backdrop of the French Revolution of 1789. The revolution began with the poor rising up against years of oppression. It was a period of great violence, which claimed the lives of the innocent and the guilty alike. In his novel, Dickens narrates the stories of people from various walks of life, who become caught up in the revolution. This extract, which introduces the main characters of the novel, begins in 1775 when a*

murderous: capable of killing

Literary term

1. This is a **transferred epithet**. The word 'murderous' describes the people who would use the guns, rather than the guns themselves.

Why did wine run down one of the streets of Saint-Antoine?

young girl travels from England to Paris to meet her father whom she had thought to be dead.

Saint-Antoine was one of the poorest parts of Paris. The children who lived there had the faces and sad voices of old men, and hunger seemed to be written on the face of every man and woman. The shops contained only the worst bits of meat and only the cheapest loaves. Nothing brightened the streets except the shops that sold tools or weapons; these contained the sharpest of bright knives and the most **murderous** of guns,[1] shining weapons that seemed to be waiting for the time when they would be brought out to do their terrible work.

A large barrel of wine had been dropped and broken in one of the streets of Saint-Antoine. Red wine began to run over through stones. Little pools of it formed in the hollows and cracks among the stones.

Immediately, everyone left whatever they were doing and ran to the spot to collect some of the wine before it disappeared into the ground. Some knelt down and tried to drink it from their hands, but most of it ran through their fingers. Some brought cups and tried to fill them; others dipped cloths in the wine and then put them in their mouths. For a time, in that street of poor and miserable people, the joyful sound of laughter rang out. But soon all the wine was gone; the laughter died down and the people returned to what they had been doing before.

A tall man dipped his finger in some mud made red with the wine and wrote on the wall five big letters: BLOOD.

The barrel of wine had been on its way to the wine shop at the corner. Outside stood the owner of the shop, **Monsieur** Defarge. He was a strongly built man of about thirty, with a face that was good-natured on the whole, but which showed signs of strong determination and a complete absence of any kind of weakness. He was a man who would be an enemy to be feared.

Monsieur Defarge stood looking at the struggle for the wine for some time. 'It isn't my affair,' he said to himself. 'As that barrel *is* broken, they must bring me another.' Then his eye caught sight of the man who had written the terrible word on the wall. He called to him: 'Say, Gaspard, are you crazy? Why do you write in the public street? Are there no better places to write such words?'

Madame Defarge was sitting in the shop when her husband re-entered it. She was a woman of about his own age, with a very keen eye, a strong face and a great calmness of manner. As her husband came in, she gave a little cough and looked in a certain direction as if to call his attention to some people who had just come into the shop.

The shopkeeper looked around until his eye rested on an oldish gentleman and a young woman who were seated in a corner. There were other people in the shop, but only these two were strangers. As he passed, he noticed that the old man attracted the attention of his young companion as if to say, 'This is our man.'

'What on earth are those two doing there?' said Defarge to himself. 'I don't know them.'

He pretended not to notice the two strangers and fell into a conversation with three men who were drinking at the bar.

Monsieur, Madame: the French words for 'Mr' and 'Mrs' respectively

signalled: showed

'How goes it, Jacques?' said one of them to Monsieur Defarge. 'Is all the wine drunk from the broken barrel?'

'Every drop of it, Jacques,' replied Defarge.

'It isn't often,' said the second man, 'that these miserable creatures know the taste of wine or of anything but black bread and death. Isn't that so, Jacques?'

'It is so, Jacques,' replied Monsieur Defarge.

A movement from Madame Defarge attracted his attention.

How did Madame Defarge draw her husband's attention?

'Gentlemen,' he said, 'the room that you wish to see is at the top of the stairs. Go into the courtyard. One of you has been there before and will show you the way.'

They paid for their wine and left. The oldish gentleman walked towards Monsieur Defarge and asked permission to speak to him. Their conversation was short. Almost at the first word, Monsieur Defarge's face showed keen attention. After a minute, Defarge **signalled** his agreement and went out. The gentleman then called to the young lady, and they, too, went outside.

Madame went on with her knitting and took no notice.

Mr Jarvis Lorry (the gentleman) and Miss Lucie Manette joined Defarge in the courtyard to which he had recently directed the three men. In the courtyard, Defarge did a surprising thing. He went down on one knee and put his lips to the young lady's hand.

Defarge at one time had been a servant of Dr Manette, Lucie's father. Lucie's mother had died and her father had disappeared: no one knew what had happened to him. His money was in Tellson's Bank – an English bank. The baby Lucie was brought to England and Mr Jarvis Lorry, an official of Tellson's Bank and an old friend of her father's, was put in charge of her money and her education.

Mr Lorry had asked an Englishwoman, Miss Pross, to bring up the child. Over the years that followed, Miss Pross became like a mother to Lucie and would have given her life for her.

Lucie was now a young woman and strange news had brought her and Mr Lorry to Paris – news that Dr Manette (who all had thought to be dead) was alive. He had been a prisoner in the Bastille, the great prison of Paris. Now he had been set free and was in the care of his old servant, Defarge.

Who was caring for Dr Manette?

Did You Know? History

In the eighteenth century, the cells of the Bastille were reserved for upper-class criminals, political prisoners and spies. Most prisoners were imprisoned without a trial. On 14 July, 1789, French revolutionaries stormed the Bastille. This was the start of the French Revolution.

Defarge rose to his feet. A remarkable change had come over his face. A look of anger and hatred had replaced his good-natured expression – hatred for those who had harmed someone he loved. 'The stairs are high,' said Defarge. 'Let us go up slowly.'

'Is Dr Manette alone?' whispered Mr Lorry.

'Of course. He has been used to being alone for so long that now he cannot bear the presence of others.'

'Is he greatly changed?'

'Changed! You will not recognise him.'

As they neared the top of the stairs, Defarge took a key out of his pocket.

'Do you keep his door locked?'

'I think it safer to do so.'

'Why?'

'Why! Because he has lived so long locked up that he would be frightened if his door were left open.'

'Is it possible?' asked Mr Lorry in surprise.

'It is possible,' replied Defarge bitterly. 'In this beautiful world, such things are possible, and not only possible, they are actually done every day.[2] Such is the state of France.'

This conversation had been held in so low a whisper that none of it reached the young lady's ears, but as they neared the top of the stairs, she was shaking.

'Courage, my dear! Courage! The worst will be over in a minute. Think only of the happiness you will bring him,' Mr Lorry said.

Literary term

2. This is an example of **irony**. Defarge says that it is a beautiful world, but he actually means that it is a terrible world where such cruel things happen to people.

As last they were near the top. Suddenly, at a turn in the stairs, they came upon the three men who were looking into a room through the cracks in a door. Hearing footsteps they turned and rose: they were the three men who had been drinking in the wine shop.

'Leave us, men. We have business here,' said Defarge.

The three went quietly down.

Mr Lorry was angry. He whispered to Defarge, 'Do you make a show of Monsieur Manette?'

'I show him to a few, to those to whom the sight is likely to do good. They are all men of my own name, Jacques. You are English and do not understand. Stay here a minute, please.'

Defarge ran his key along the door as if to give a warning to the person inside. Then, he put it in the lock and turned it slowly. The door opened; he looked into the room and said something.

What did Defarge do with his key and why?

A faint voice answered. Defarge looked back and signalled to them to enter. Mr Lorry put his arm round Lucie's waist and held her. 'Go in,' he said. 'Go in.'

'I am afraid,' she answered, still shaking.

'Afraid of what?'

'I am afraid of him, my father.'

He pulled her arm around his neck, lifted her a little and hurried into the room.

Work was going on in the room. With his back towards the door and his face towards the window, a white-haired man sat on a long bench, bent forward. He was very busy, making shoes.

About the author

Charles Dickens (1812–1870), an English novelist, is regarded as one of the greatest writers of the nineteenth century. His works are loved for their realistic depiction of Victorian England, their comedy, and concern for social reform. *Great Expectations*, *David Copperfield* and *Oliver Twist* are some of his most popular novels.

Comprehension

Quick Recap

A. Answer the questions with reference to context.

1. *'Why do you write in the public street? Are there no better places to write such words?'*
   a. Who said these words and to whom?
   b. Describe the speaker's appearance.

c. What had the person spoken to written in the public street? What did he use to write it?

2. *'Gentlemen, the room that you wish to see is at the top of the stairs.'*
   a. Who said these words and to whom? Who was in the room?
   b. Why was the speaker taking other people to the room?
   c. What was Mr Lorry's reaction to this action of the speaker?

3. *'I'm afraid of him, my father'.*
   a. Who said these words? Where was the speaker at the time?
   b. Why was the speaker afraid?
   c. What was the speaker's father doing when she saw him?
   d. Who was the speaker travelling with? How did this person reassure her?

B. Answer the questions in a few lines.

1. Describe the condition of the street in Saint-Antoine. Which were the only shops on the street that did good business?
2. Which incident changed the mood of the street?
3. Describe Madame Defarge.
4. Who was Lucie Manette? What role did Jarvis Lorry play in her life?
5. Where had Lucie been brought up and by whom? Why was she in Paris?
6. Why did Defarge and one of his visitors address each other as 'Jacques'?
7. Why did Defarge kiss Lucie's hand?
8. Why was Dr Manette alone? Why did Defarge always keep his room locked?

Life Skills and Values sympathy for the downtrodden, adaptability

Think and answer.

1. Why do you think Gaspard wrote the word 'blood' on the wall? Why did Defarge suggest that he should write it somewhere else?
2. What kind of people were Monsieur and Madame Defarge? Give examples from the passage to support your answer.

21ST CENTURY Critical Thinking

Way with Words

TRANSFORMATION OF PARTS OF SPEECH

A. Change the forms of these words from the passage, according to the instructions.

1. poor (noun)
2. keen (noun)
3. pretended (noun)
4. fear (adjective)
5. recognise (noun)
6. conversation (verb)
7. terrible (verb)
8. bitterly (noun)
9. disappeared (noun)
10. public (adverb)
11. pool (verb)
12. young (noun)

B. The words in each of the following sets have the same general meaning. But they differ in their specific meanings. Write the meanings of the words based on the given criteria.

1. run	jog	scamper	(speed of movement)
2. flow	trickle	gush	(intensity of movement of water)
3. terrible	dreadful	miserable	(an act)
4. wave	gesture	signal	(to make a sign)

Grammar in Use

Transformation of Sentences

We can rewrite sentences in various ways without changing their meaning.

1. using 'too ... to' and 'so ... that' interchangeably
   Example: This barrel of wine is **so** heavy **that** I cannot carry it.
   The sentence can be written as: This barrel of wine is **too** heavy for me **to** carry.
   Note that if the sentence with 'so ... that' is negative (with **not** in it), then the sentence with 'too ... to' will always be positive.
2. by replacing the phrase, 'in case' with the conjunction 'lest' and vice versa
   Example: Please speak softly **in case** the young lady overhears you.
   The sentence can be written as: Please speak softly **lest** the young lady overhears you.
3. using the subjunctive mood
   We use the subjunctive mood to express a wish, a suggestion, a command or an imaginary situation. In the subjunctive form, verbs take their base form and do not change on the basis of person or number.
   Examples: I *wish* I **were** able to explain the problem to you.
   She *suggested* that Matthew **work** full time instead of staying at home.

   The verbs most often used with the subjunctive are **wish**, **suggest**, **ask**, **command**, **demand**, **insist**, **order** and **recommend**.

A. Rewrite the sentences according to the instructions.

1. The news is too good to be true. (rewrite using 'so ... that')
2. I want the doctor to begin the operation now. (begin: I insist that ...)
3. Helga took the prisoner outside the city gates. The prisoner might have been spotted in the city. (join the sentences using 'lest')
4. The king is so popular that he will not be dethroned. (rewrite using 'too ... to')
5. The shy young man spent the whole day in his room. He did not want to trouble his hosts. (join the sentences using 'lest')
6. If I had been a butterfly, I would have had wings. (begin: If I were ...)
7. It's too risky to start a new business after the recent financial crisis. It would be best not to try it. (rewrite using 'so ... that')
8. Kristen baked an extra cake for the party in case they fell short. (rewrite using 'lest')

Adjectives: Changing Degrees of Comparison

You know that adjectives have three degrees of comparison: positive, comparative and superlative.

Look at these sentences.

> No other sport in the world is **as popular as** football. (positive)
> Football is **more popular than** all other sports in the world. (comparative)
> Football is the **most popular** sport in the world. (superlative)

Each sentence uses a different degree of comparison for the adjective **popular**, without changing the meaning.

Now, look at these sentences.

> Saint-Antoine was **one of the poorest** parts of Paris.
> **No other part** of Paris was **as poor as** Saint-Antoine. (incorrect)
> Saint-Antoine was **poorer than most** other parts of Paris. (correct)

The phrase 'one of the ...' cannot be rewritten using the structure 'no other ...' because the person or idea being compared (Saint-Antoine) is not the only one of its kind.

B. Rewrite the sentences according to the instructions.

1. Madhu is the most melodious singer in her school. (change to comparative degree)
2. No other school has a larger campus than ours. (change to positive degree)
3. Delhi is more polluted than any other city in north India. (change to superlative degree)
4. No other flower smells as sweet as the rose. (change to comparative degree)
5. India is one of the largest democracies in the world. (change to comparative degree)
6. William Shakespeare is one of the most famous dramatists of the world. (change to comparative degree)
7. Kolkata is more densely populated than most other cities in India. (begin: Very few ...)
8. Kunal is the cleverest boy in the class. (change to positive degree)

Study Skills

Pronounce Well

You know that many words have different pronunciations even though they are spelt with the same vowels and/or consonants.
Examples: dr**ought** (rhymes with 'doubt') and f**ought** (rhymes with 'ought')

You also know that words with similar pronunciation are often spelt with different vowels.
Examples: bet, lead

Strike out the word with the odd pronunciation in each of the following sets. One is done for you.

1. *choose*	*lose*	~~*fuse*~~	*ruse*	*blues*
2. owl	bowl	soul	mole	goal

3. rummage	wreckage	fuselage	garbage	damage
4. blew	grew	sew	blue	drew
5. wear	rear	bear	pear	rare
6. meat	beat	neat	seat	threat
7. tough	rough	stuff	bough	cough
8. jeopardy	leopard	shepherd	weapon	people

Listening and Speaking

Listen to a short passage about a sudden mishap. Now, imagine that you are sitting in Monsieur Defarge's shop, when the strange events unfold in the street outside. Describe what you see.

Use the phrases you heard in the passage and the ones below to describe the scene.

This happened when ...	Before long ...	This was followed by ...
The next thing I knew ...	All of a sudden ...	Finally ...

Pen it Down

If you could go back in time and be a part of an incident that changed the course of history, which event would you choose to be a part of? What would your role in it be? Write an essay on the topic and give it a suitable title.

You can use the following points in your account:

- how the event affected the world
- why you would want to be a part of it and your reasons for choosing the role
- anything you would like to change about the event

Self Assessment

Now I can

- understand the suffering of the common citizens in eighteenth-century France.
- see how families were separated due to the cruelty of the aristocracy.
- practise transformation of sentences using *too ... to*, *so ... that*, *lest*, *I wish I were*, and understand the comparison of adjectives.
- understand the difference between general and specific meanings of words, describe a scene and write an essay.

Research and Write

A. Both 'The River Came Home' and 'Felling of the Banyan Tree' describe the sense of loss felt by youngsters. This is symbolised by a tree in both stories.

Compare the situation of the main characters in both the texts and the way they deal with their loss.

B. In the poem 'Where the Mind is Without Fear', Tagore dreams of a country where people are free in every respect. Democracy is considered to be the most progressive form of government, where the citizens are free to choose their own leaders.

Do you think India is a truly democratic country? Write an essay on the topic, correlating it with the ideas included in the poem. Include examples from the present day to illustrate your points.

C. The poem 'The Road Not Taken' is as much about the choices we make, as the choices we walk away from.

Write a short story about how a choice not made had a lasting impact on the life of the protagonist. Give a suitable title to your story.

D. 'A Tale of Two Cities' is set during the French Revolution of 1789, which is considered to be one of the most important events in that century.

Which, according to you, has been the most significant event of the twenty-first century so far? Write a factual essay about the event, explaining why you think it is the most significant.

7

Ozymandias

Percy Bysshe Shelley

Let's Get Started

A. Collect images for these categories and paste them side by side in your notebook, as a way of contrasting the past and the present.

1. family portraits
2. modes of land or air transport
3. houses
4. advertisements

What did you notice about the differences between the images in each category? Why did these differences occur? What changes with time? Form groups in class and discuss.

B. Work in pairs and choose any ancient monument which is now in ruins, for example, the Colosseum in Rome, the Nalanda University in Bihar, or the ruins of the Inca civilisation in Machu Picchu. Research and write a short paragraph describing what it must have looked like in its own age. Remember to use appropriate adjectives in your paragraph.

21ST CENTURY Information Literacy

HC **Learning and Awareness:** Understanding of the self, existence and universal human behaviour

Reading

This poem is inspired by a statue of the Egyptian pharaoh, Rameses II. Composed as a

traveller's account, it shows that even the mightiest kings and empires decline and fade away with time.

I met a traveller from an **antique** land
Who said: 'Two vast and trunkless legs of stone
Stand in the desert. Near them, on the sand,
Half sunk, a **shattered visage** lies, whose frown,
And wrinkled lip, and **sneer** of cold **command**,
Tell that its sculptor well those **passions read**
Which yet survive, **stamped** on these lifeless things,
The hand that **mocked** them, and the heart that fed;[1]
And on the **pedestal** these words appear:
'My name is Ozymandias, king of kings,
Look on my works, ye mighty, and despair!'
Nothing beside remains.[2] Round the decay
Of that **colossal** wreck, boundless and bare
The lone and level sands stretch far away.'

Whom did the poet meet?

Literary terms

1. This is a **synecdoche**. The 'hand' stands for the artist, who sculpted the statue, imitating perfectly the facial expressions of Ozymandias. The heart stands for the king whose emotions are still visible in the half-ruined face of the statue.

2. This is an example of **irony**. The words on the base of the statue, which were meant to inspire fear and awe about the powerful king, are a stark contrast to its actual state of ruin.

antique: ancient
shattered visage: broken face
sneer: expression showing scorn
command: authority
passions: intense emotions
read: understood
stamped: marked
mocked: (here) copied
pedestal: the base on which a statue is mounted
colossal: enormous

About the poet

Percy Bysshe Shelley (1792–1822) was one of the major English Romantic poets. He was considered controversial for writing on themes like atheism and non-violent resistance. His poetry was recognised only after his death. Some of his best-loved poems are 'Ode to the West Wind' and 'To a Skylark'.

Comprehension

Quick Recap

A. Answer the questions in a few lines.

1. Where had the traveller come from?
2. What had he seen in the desert? What are the various phrases used to describe it in the poem?
3. What was written on the pedestal of the statue? Explain it in your own words. What do the lines say about the character of Ozymandias?
4. Who are the two narrators in the poem?

B. Answer the questions with reference to context.

1. *Near them, on the sand,/Half sunk, a shattered visage lies*
   a. Who is the speaker in these lines?
   b. What was the expression on the face of the statue? What did the expression say about the sculptor?
   c. Explain the meaning of the phrase 'shattered visage'. Why was it half sunk?
2. *The hand that mocked them, and the heart that fed;*
   a. Whose hand is being referred to in the given line? Who does the word 'them' refer to?
   b. Explain the two meanings of the word 'mocked'.
   c. Whose heart is being referred to in the line? What had it 'fed'?
   d. Where do the passions of the old king survive?
3. *Nothing beside remains. Round the decay/Of that colossal wreck, boundless and bare/ The lone and level sands stretch far away.*
   a. Explain the line 'Nothing beside remains'. What does it say about Ozymandias' attempt to make people 'despair' when they saw the statue?
   b. What is the meaning of the phrase 'colossal wreck'?
   c. Describe the landscape around the statue of Ozymandias.
   d. Mention three examples of alliteration in the given lines.

Life Skills and Values — appreciating imagery, time as a great leveller

Think and answer.

1. How does the poet create the impression of a faraway and ancient land in the poem?
2. Do you think the traveller was awed by the statue of Ozymandias? Give reasons for your answer. (21st Century Critical Thinking)
3. What is the message of the poem? Is it relevant in today's world?

HC Exploring maintenance of balance in orders

Way with Words

Metonymy

You have seen the use of synecdoche in the poem.

Metonymy is a similar figure of speech in which we use a closely connected feature of something in place of the thing itself.

Example: The city gates were bravely defended by the **rifles**.
Here, the word 'rifles' refers to the guards who held the rifles.

A. Identify and explain the use of metonymy in these sentences.

1. The pen is mightier than the sword.
2. Friends, Romans, countrymen, lend me your ears.
3. She works for an important newspaper.
4. The library has been quite helpful to students.
5. She is planning to serve the dish quite early in the evening.
6. He was lucky to get a job on Wall Street as soon as he graduated from college.

Words Indicating Size

The poem uses the words 'vast', 'colossal' and 'boundless' to show how large the statue of Ozymandias was.

B. Write the following synonyms for big or small in the correct columns. Use a dictionary for words whose meanings you might not know.

big	small

gargantuan	meagre
minuscule	mammoth
inconsiderable	mountainous
titanic	slight
minor	ample

Idioms with *Hand* and *Heart*

C. In the poem, you came across the line 'The hand that mocked them and the heart that fed'. Match these idioms and phrases with hand and heart with their correct meanings.

Idiom	Meaning
1. hand in glove •	• a. make or lose money very quickly
2. heart of gold •	• b. (of a conversation) honest and personal
3. hand over fist •	• c. deeply felt, sincere
4. heart of the matter •	• d. very kind
5. heartfelt •	• e. the central point of an issue
6. heart-to-heart •	• f. in close association with

Grammar in Use

Prepositions

You know that **prepositions** show the relation between a noun or a pronoun and other words in a sentence. They can give more information about time, place and movement.

Examples: I met the traveller **at** noon. (preposition of time)
Two vast and trunkless legs of stone/Stand **in** the desert. (preposition of place)
The ruins spread **across** the length of the desert. (preposition of movement)

A. Rewrite the sentences by changing the incorrect prepositions. Delete the ones that are unnecessary. (There may be more than one answer for some sentences.)

1. Uma goes home on bus.
2. A fool is easily parted of his money.
3. The forests of the Amazon abound with flora and fauna.
4. When we leave to college after school, it is hard to part of friends.
5. Can we keep this information among ourselves?
6. I am going to a hike this weekend.
7. I haven't met Sheila since more than a week.
8. I am not allowed to leave school since the end of the day.

Combining Prepositions with Verbs and Adjectives

Phrasal verbs are commonly formed by combining a verb and a preposition.
Examples: A thief **broke into** Shreyas' flat yesterday. (forcibly entered)
Jamie **broke out** in a rash a day before the annual concert. (developed)

We also use adjectives and prepositions together to form prepositional phrases.
Examples: Are you **aware of** the taxi strike tomorrow?
My sister is **fond of** trekking. She goes for a trek to the Himalayas every year.

B. Complete the sentences with the correct prepositions.

1. The ship was bound ________ the tropical islands.
2. I cannot comply ________ your wishes anymore.
3. The accused was convicted ________ the crime.
4. She had many servants attending ________ her.
5. When no help arrived a week after the hurricane, the inhabitants reconciled themselves ________ their fates.
6. A sincere student is never negligent ________ his studies.
7. The house was infested ________ rodents.
8. Her face looks familiar ________ me.

Study Skills

Pronounce Well

You have learnt about stressed and unstressed syllables. The combination of stressed and unstressed syllables in poetry is known as a **foot**.

The arrangement of feet in a regular structure or pattern is called **metre**. Foot is the unit of metre. A foot consisting of an unstressed syllable followed by a stressed one is called an **iamb**. The iamb is the most common metre in poetry.

Look at these lines from the poem with the stressed syllables in bold, and each foot marked with a stroke.

I **met**/a **trav**/eller **from**/an **an**/tique **land**
Who **said**,/Two **vast**/and **trunk**/less **legs**/of **stone**

A. Listen to the stanzas given below and do the following:

1. **Divide the words in each line into syllables using a hyphen.**
2. **Underline the stressed syllables.**
3. **Mark each foot with a stroke. Note the iambic pattern of alternating stressed and unstressed syllables.**

Stand in the desert. Near them, on the sand,
Half sunk, a shattered visage lies, whose frown,
And wrinkled lip, and sneer of cold command,
Tell that its sculptor well those passions read
Which yet survive, stamped on these lifeless things,
The hand that mocked them, and the heart that fed;

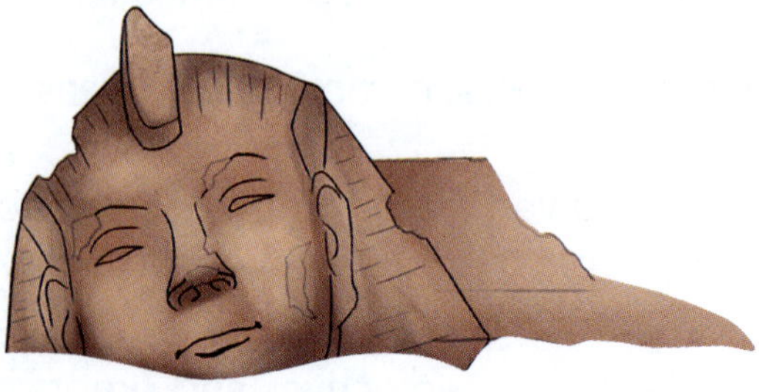

And on the pedestal these words appear:
'My name is Ozymandias, king of kings,
Look on my works, ye mighty, and despair!'
Nothing beside remains. Round the decay
Of that colossal wreck, boundless and bare
The lone and level sands stretch far away.'

Listening and Speaking

Is it more important to look for wealth and fame in life or to try to be better human beings? Form two groups and express your opinion on either of the two points of view.

21ST CENTURY Communication

You can use the following points in the debate:

For

- History shows that wealth and fame do not last.
- People remember the good deeds we do for them.

Against

- It is human nature to want better lives for ourselves.
- Wealth can enable us to help others.

Pen it Down

Imagine that you are an ancient monument, built to celebrate an important event. But the neglected monument is in ruins today. Write an autobiography describing your journey from splendour to misery. You can use the following points in the autobiography:

- the event that inspired the monument
- how the passage of time and historical events have affected the monument
- efforts to restore it

21ST CENTURY Creativity

Self Assessment

Now I can

- understand that we should not be vain about our achievements because time brings everything to an end.
- understand synecdoche and metonymy, use prepositions and prepositional phrases.
- learn about metre and feet in poetry, participate in a debate and write an autobiography.

Read More

Death the Leveller: This poem by James Shirley is about the power of death to remove distinctions between the rich and the poor, including the king with his crown and the peasant with his spade.

King Canute: This poem by William Makepeace Thackeray is about the legendary Scottish king who, at the end of a long reign, is weary and wishes for death. He teaches his flattering courtiers, who insist he will never die, that even a king is subject to the laws of nature.

Environment

8

The Monk Protectors of Arunachal's Wetlands

Ranju Dodum

SUSTAINABLE DEVELOPMENT GOALS

Let's Get Started

15 LIFE ON LAND

The United Nations Sustainable Development Goal 15 talks about preserving life on land by restoring ecosystems such as forests, wetlands, grasslands, drylands and mountains. The more aware we are about the environment around us, the better prepared we can be to care for it.

Read the clues and solve this crossword on words related to the environment.

Across

4. the natural environment where an animal or plant lives or grows
5. areas of very wet, muddy land with wild plants growing in it
6. breaks down or decays naturally
7. protection of the environment
9. plants or animals who have the same main traits
10. practice of providing holidays and related services that do not harm the environment

Down

1. the ability to be maintained at a steady level without exhausting natural resources
2. describes those whose survival is threatened
3. all the animals living in an area
8. the study of relationships between living beings and their environment

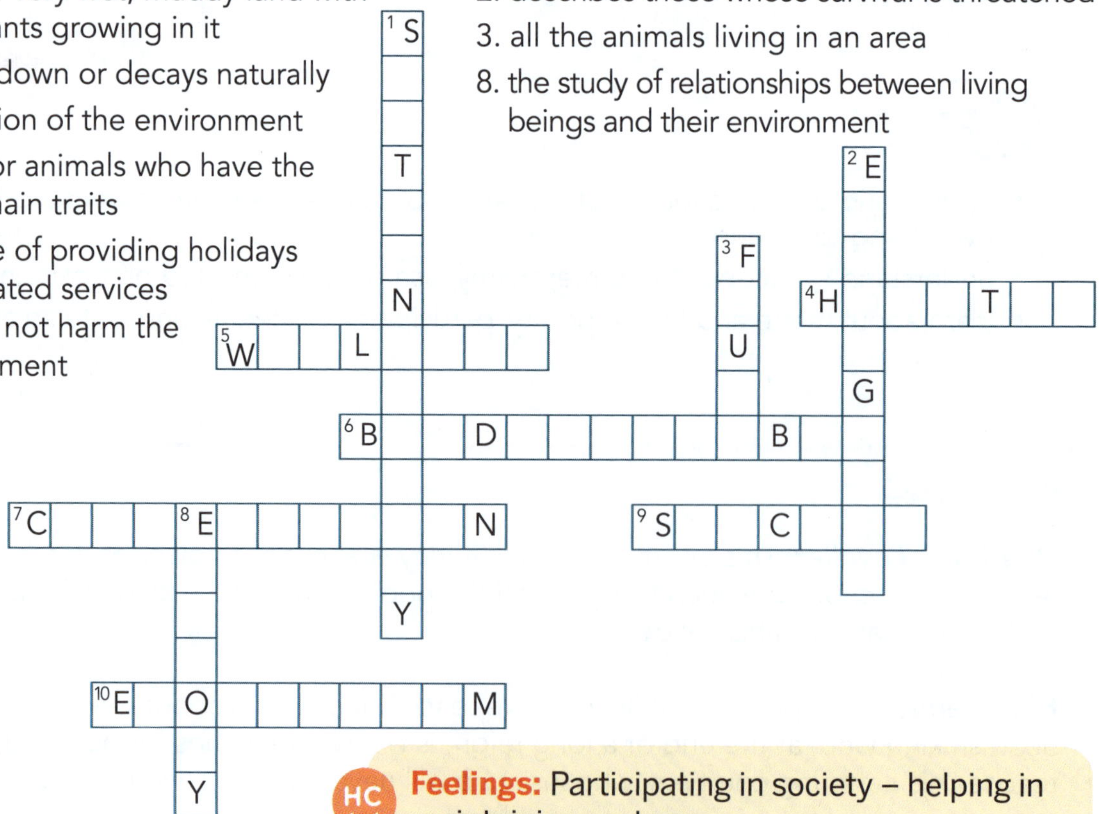

Feelings: Participating in society – helping in maintaining systems

Reading

Have you ever planted a tree, or cared for a tree growing in your neighbourhood? Read this account to see how the selfless actions of individuals and groups have contributed towards protection of the environment and its biodiversity.

Seated on a carpet on the floor of the Buddhist **monastery** in Itanagar, Phuntsok Wangchuk cuts a lonely figure on this particular Friday morning. With a rather **flimsy** surgical mask covering his nose and mouth, the *lama* or monk, appears to still be taking Covid-19 precautionary measures when most people in Arunachal Pradesh have discarded them. Using a wooden twig, he is rolling cotton **wicks** that will be used to light oil lamps that are used to offer prayers.

Wangchuk is a Buddhist monk from the Monpa tribe that traditionally lives in the West Kameng and Tawang districts of the state. The Monpas are the main **ethnic** group in Arunachal Pradesh, known for their skills in wood carving, and carpet and cloth-weaving. Scattered groups of the tribe are also said to reside across international borders in Bhutan and China. For centuries, the Monpa have been followers of Tibetan Buddhism. Tawang houses the largest monastery of Tibetan Buddhism in the country and is second in size only to the Potala Palace in Lhasa, Tibet.

monastery: a building or collection of buildings in which monks live

flimsy: badly made

wicks: pieces of string in candles which burn when they are lit

ethnic: connected with or relating to a particular racial or cultural group of people

standard-issue: the basic equipment or clothing that is given to all the members of a particular group

Founded in around 1680-81, the Tawang Monastery's Tibetan name is *Gaden Namgyal Lhatse*. It was affiliated to the Drepung Monastery in Tibet until the Chinese occupation. Located at around 3,000 metres above sea level, the monastery's complex reportedly houses around 500 monks. The monastery also owns large herds of livestock, including yaks.

Tawang Monastery

Having spent two months in the town of Tawang, the administrative headquarters of the district with the same name, Wangchuk is now in the state capital Itanagar and living at the compound of the *gompa* or monastery.

At this particular time today, he is alone inside the *gompa*. 'The other *lamas* have gone to the chief minister's house to perform a religious ceremony,' he informs us.

Dressed in the **standard-issue** maroon/orange-hued clothing, he seems blissfully unaware of the importance of the environmental work he does for three months of the year.

What skills are the Monpas known for?

Did You Know? Geography

Wetlands, a type of land ecosystem, are naturally wet either permanently or seasonally. They act as natural water filters by trapping pollutants like phosphorous, heavy metals and harmful gases in their soil.

Over the past 14 years, Phuntsok Wangchuk has spent around three months every year at the Bhagajang Wetland Complex to guide and care for pilgrims who visit the sacred wetlands in Arunachal Pradesh.

The sacred wetlands

Arunachal Pradesh has 1672 high altitude wetlands (above 3000 metres altitude). They are among the highest such wetlands in India, after Kashmir.

At an elevation of above 4,000 metres in Tawang district lies the Bhagajang Wetland Complex. It has around 20 high-altitude lakes ranging from 0.01 square kilometres to about 0.35 square kilometres. At least 12 of these are considered sacred by Buddhist communities and have their own folklore.

Bhagajang and other wetland complexes in the state act as reservoirs for the three major rivers — Tawangchu, Nyamjangchu and Kameng River, which are important tributaries of the Brahmaputra.

A sacred lake in Arunachal Pradesh

Bordering West Kameng in the south and Bhutan to the west, the wetland complex is around 18 kilometres from the national highway on Sela Pass — a **strategic** mountain pass connecting Tawang district to the rest of India.

How far is the wetland complex from Sela Pass?

The **rugged** mountains and the thick forested areas of Arunachal Pradesh, coupled with bad road infrastructure, mean that distance is measured not in kilometres but in hours for the people who live here.

'There is a road and it takes around seven hours to reach from Sela Pass,' the *lama* says, rolling more cotton wicks.

The Buddhists celebrate *Asalha Puja* or *Dharma Day* in August and September and thousands of pilgrims make a **gruelling** journey to the *gompa* at Bhagajang. Since 2006, Wangchuk has spent around three months from August to October every year at the Complex to guide and care for the pilgrims who visit the site during that small window of time when the road and the area are not covered in snow. The entire complex is held in religious reverence and there are images of deities painted on stones and boulders in the area.

Wangchuk says that the pilgrims come from the two districts of Arunachal Pradesh as well as Bhutan for an

strategic: relating to the most important, general aspects of something

rugged: uneven and covered with rocks, with few trees or plants

gruelling: extremely difficult and tiring

Wordwise

The phrase *window of time* literally refers to a period of time, with a definite start and end, within which a particular thing can be done.

annual pilgrimage. In 2021, the Bhutanese pilgrims could not come because of Covid-19 travel restrictions.

During the three-month period when pilgrims come and go, there are usually two or three monks who stay there, as do the *Brokpa* — yak herders among the Monpa — who bring their livestock to graze in the area.

As we converse, he speaks little about the environmental protection work that the monastery is doing.

Monks team up with conservation group

Arunachal Pradesh gets an average of 1.9 million tourists each year (domestic and foreign), per the official tourism survey of 2014-15. Of this number, Tawang district gets more than 150,000 visitors annually. There is no official record of the number of visitors at Bhagajang specifically, though individual estimates peg it between 400-1000 visitors per year.

Did You Know? G.K.

The yak is a long-haired cattle found throughout the Himalayan region of the Indian subcontinent, the Tibetan Plateau, and as far north as Mongolia and Siberia.

The concerns about the impact of tourism on the environment however, came up over a decade ago. In August 2009, officials from the Tawang Monastery and World Wildlife Fund (WWF) India agreed to a partnership to address some of these issues. According to WWF India, some of the threats to the region included inadequate **infrastructure** and resources to support the increasing number of pilgrims visiting these lakes, the cutting of vegetation patches to use for fuel, increase in pressure on the grazing grounds, among others.

Officials from the Tawang Monastery decided to put an immediate ban on the cutting of firewood from the area, and WWF India promised to provide high-efficiency kerosene stoves to the monastery which would be used by visitors for cooking during their stay.

How would the kerosene stoves be used?

Strict regulations were put in place to ensure that visitors carrying food packed in non-biodegradable packets would return with the waste. If they were left with bio-degradable waste, they would use dustbins (provided by WWF) in various places for disposal. Specific sites were designated for camping, and WWF would help construct toilets near these sites.

infrastructure: the basic systems and services that are necessary for a system or organisation to run smoothly

defecation: the act of getting rid of solid waste from one's body

Kamal Medhi, the Landscape Coordinator for the WWF's Western Arunachal Landscape programme, says that many of those agreements have been fulfilled. Dustbins have been placed in the area. Kerosene stoves were given to the monastery in 2012, with the fuel provided by the district administration.

To ease living conditions around Bhagajang, the WWF also provided tents and water tanks, and built toilets to address the issue of open **defecation**.

Another problem was the offering of *khadas*—a silky traditional scarf of religious significance—being thrown into the lakes and having an **adverse** impact on the ecology of the complex. Medhi said this was resolved to an extent by building wooden hangers across the lakes to which pilgrims could tie the *khadas*, instead of throwing them in the lake.

Such measures form conservation in action in a very difficult terrain. In remote areas like Arunachal Pradesh, conservation of the local flora and fauna cannot take place without the trust and involvement of the people living there.

The WWF also lists a lack of awareness about the value of the wetlands as a concern. The community-based tourism happening in Bhagajang is a way to solve this problem.

Speaking from his residence in Tezpur in Assam, Medhi feels that there is a need to **revamp** the approach to protection of the ecosystem. 'The local community should view these steps not just as a means to preserve religious practices, but also consider the environmental importance of taking these measures,' he says.

Bhagajang is a typical high-altitude wetland. Here, trees thin out and soon disappear completely. The wetlands are found in the area between the tree cover and the start of the **snow line**. They are a mix of meadows, marshland and waterbodies which support an incredible richness of flora and fauna, making it a **biodiversity hotspot**. Rhododendron, juniper shrubs, along with a variety to medicinal plants thrive in the region. Around 78 plant species have been recorded in a WWF-India study in 2013-14. The study also showed the presence of endangered species such as the musk deer, the Asiatic wild dog and the red fox in Bhagajang.

Which endangered animals can be found in Bhagajang?

In 2014, a camera trap setup by the WWF even captured images of a leopard cat at an elevation of 4,250 metres, making it the highest recorded sighting of the animal at that time in India.

Researchers have documented records of sightings of several other animals including the **elusive** red panda. Wangchuk, who has been going there for the past 14 years and was

adverse: unfavourable

revamp: make changes to something in order to try and improve it

snow line: the height above which snow never melts completely

biodiversity hotspot: a region which has many species of plants and animals, and which is endangered, usually as a result of human activities

elusive: difficult to find

there even during the pandemic last year, has sighted many migratory birds.

'We see *ngangapa* and *aakpu*,' he says, using the local names of bird species, many of whom are only found here. Almost as **nonchalantly**, he says he has also seen *junglee billi* (wild cat)—that could mean anything from a leopard to a **civet**.

nonchalantly: in a calm and relaxed manner

civet: a catlike wild animal found mainly in parts of Africa and Asia

Having been a regular visitor to the wetlands, Wangchuk says that it is expected of him to go this year too. Eight years ago, his friend and travelling partner, Nawang Tashi, had died. Wangchuk might just make one more trip this year too.

Comprehension

Quick Recap

A. Read the statements and say whether they are true (T) or false (F). Correct the false statements.

1. Phuntsok Wangchuk belongs to the Monpa tribe.
2. The Brahmaputra is a tributary of the Tawangchu.
3. The Buddhists celebrate *Asalha Puja* or *Dharma Day* in August and September.
4. People come from three districts of Arunachal Pradesh as well as Bhutan for an annual pilgrimage to the *gompa* at Bhagajang.
5. Officials from the Tawang Monastery have put a ban on the cutting of firewood from the area.
6. Community based tourism is prevalent in Bhagajang.

B. Answer the questions with reference to context.

1. *Using a wooden twig, he is rolling cotton wicks...*
   a. Who is referred to as 'he' in this sentence?
   b. Where was he? Why was he rolling cotton wicks?
   c. What environmental work does he do for three months of the year?
2. *'There is a road and it takes around seven hours to reach from Sela Pass,'*
   a. Who said these words?
   b. What takes around seven hours to reach?
   c. What was peculiar about the way the speaker talks about the distance to the place?
   d. Why do you think the speaker uses this particular method to talk about distances?
3. *The concerns about the impact of tourism on the environment however, came up over a decade ago.*
   a. What were the concerns about the impact of tourism?
   b. Who decided to form a partnership to address some of these issues?
   c. What changes did they bring about?

4. *'We see* ngangapa *and* aakpu,'...
   a. Who said these words?
   b. What are 'ngangapa' and 'aakpu'? Where can they be seen?
   c. What else did the speaker reportedly see?

Life Skills and Values following safety precautions, eco-tourism, conservation

Think and answer.

1. Why do you think it is important to follow safety protocols during a pandemic?
2. How is community-based tourism in Bhagajang building awareness about the value of the wetlands? What are the benefits of eco-tourism in protecting the environment and culture of a place?
3. How does the involvement of locals help in conservation of the environment? Explain your answer with examples from the passage.

Way with Words

Collocations

In English, some words are often used together to create a distinct meaning. Such groups of words are called **collocations**.

Example: blissfully unaware
This phrase means 'the state of not knowing about something and so being unable to worry about it'.

Fill in the blanks with the collocations given in the box.

cut a lonely figure	adverse impact	offer prayers
flora and fauna	put in place	captured images

1. The people decided to ______________ in memory of the soldiers who died in the battlefield.
2. The ______________ of a particular region are the plants and animals that can be found there.
3. The naughty boy was ______________ by the clever teacher.
4. The CCTV camera ______________ of the thief when he broke into the room.
5. The sole attendant at the meeting ______________ as he took his place in the front row.
6. Excessive enforcement of discipline might have an ______________ on children.

Grammar in Use

Active and Passive Voice

You know that the voice in a sentence indicates whether the subject of the sentence performed the main action or was the recipient of the action in the sentence.

A sentence in which the subject is the doer of the action is said to be in the **active voice**.

Example: The Buddhists celebrate *Asalha Puja* or *Dharma Day* in August and September.

A sentence in which the subject of the sentence is the recipient of the action is said to be in the **passive voice**.

Example: *Asalha Puja* or *Dharma Day* is celebrated by the Buddhists in August and September.

When we change a sentence from active to passive, the subject in the active voice becomes the object in the passive voice and vice versa. Usually, the agent in the passive voice is introduced by the preposition **by**. The doer of the action may be left out in the passive voice if it is not important.

Example: Specific sites were designated for camping. (passive)
(They) designated specific sites for camping. (active)

Also, remember that intransitive verbs cannot be converted to the passive form because they do not have an object.

Example: Wangchuk is alone inside the gompa. (*is*: intransitive verb)

Now, look at this table that shows how tenses are changed from active to passive voice.

Tense	Simple	Continuous	Perfect
Present			
Active voice	Wangchuk **cares** for the pilgrims.	Wangchuk **is caring** for the pilgrims.	Wangchuk **has cared** for the pilgrims.
Passive voice	The pilgrims **are cared** for by Wangchuk.	The pilgrims **are being cared** for by Wangchuk.	The pilgrims **have been cared** for by Wangchuk.
Past			
Active voice	Wangchuk **cared** for the pilgrims.	Wangchuk **was caring** for the pilgrims.	Wangchuk **had cared** for the pilgrims.
Passive voice	The pilgrims **were cared** for by Wangchuk.	The pilgrims **were being cared** for by Wangchuk.	The pilgrims **had been cared** for by Wangchuk.
Future			
Active voice	Wangchuk **will care** for the pilgrims.	Wangchuk **will be caring** for the pilgrims.	Wangchuk **will have cared** for the pilgrims.
Passive voice	The pilgrims **will be cared** for by Wangchuk.	(No passive voice)	The pilgrims **will have been cared** for by Wangchuk.

A. Rewrite these sentences according to the instructions.

1. The forest fire destroyed the entire area. (end with ... forest fire.)
2. The critic wrote an encouraging review of the film. (begin: An ...)
3. I clean the house every weekend. (begin: The house ...)
4. My advertisement for the sale was not responded to. (use: No one ...)
5. Who ate the last piece of cake? (end with ... eaten?)
6. By whom were you taught to skate? (begin: Who ...)

B. Rewrite these sentences in the passive voice. Point out the sentence in which conversion is not possible.

1. Fake news is spreading like wildfire.
2. By this time next year, scientists will be controlling the spread of the virus.
3. He bought some gym equipment to tackle his health issues.
4. I am writing a new song at the moment.
5. He swam across the English Channel.
6. The teacher taught us the poem well.

Study Skills

Pronounce Well

You know that all words have at least one stressed syllable and one or more unstressed syllables. The stressed syllable is usually marked with an apostrophe. (') The following are some patterns of stress in words with two syllables:

1. Some words with two syllables are formed by adding a suffix or prefix to the base form. **Examples:** lone**ly**, **un**tie
   In such words, the stress is on the base or main part of the word, i.e. un/tie', lone'/ly, child'/hood, eat'/ing, larg'/er, sculpt'/or, re/fresh'
2. In words with the 'uh' sound, spelt using the vowels **a**, **e**, **i**, **o**, **u**, the syllable with this sound is never stressed. **Examples:** per/form', a/lone', a/mend'

Divide these words into syllables. Then, mark the stressed syllables with an apostrophe. Say the words aloud with stress on the correct syllable.

1. garden
2. tenants
3. raven
4. handling
5. broken
6. axes
7. matter
8. passage
9. often
10. question
11. letter
12. sawing
13. open
14. aside
15. distance
16. nearly
17. weapon
18. ordered
19. poorly
20. lower

Listening and Speaking

Listen to a passage on snow leopards and fill in the blanks correctly.

endangered	climate	predator's	biodiversity
restore	landscape	shrinking	survival

The forbidding ________ of the Himalayas is home to the mysterious and elusive snow leopard. Its grey fur dotted with black spots and rosettes, this stealthy ________ silent presence is essential in maintaining the rich ________ of the area.

Snow leopards, unfortunately, are an ________ species. ________ habitat, careless poaching and drastic ________ changes predict a worrying future for this unique species.

Conservationists, local communities and the government have started several programmes to ensure the ________ of this species. These aim to ________ the snow leopard population in the areas where it used to be abundantly found.

Pen it Down

A **précis** is a summary of a text or speech. It briefly states the important facts, leaving out lengthy descriptions and examples.

These are the steps you should follow while writing a précis:

- Read the passage well and understand what the focus is.
- Write the important points and make an outline. Leave out repetitions and examples.
- Draw a grid on the basis of the total number of words allowed.
- Use a pencil to write the précis by filling the words in the grid using the outline. Be careful not to exceed the word limit.
- Make a fair draft of the rough version, and mention the number of words used.
- Give a suitable title to your précis.

Write a précis in not more than fifty words about the measures that have been taken by the Tawang Monastery and the WWF to ease the impact of tourism on the environment of the wetlands.

Self Assessment

Now I can

- understand the importance of people's efforts towards conservation of the environment.
- use collocations, and practise using the active and passive voice.
- identify stressed syllables, listen and fill in the gaps and write a précis.

9

Elder Brother

Munshi Premchand

Let's Get Started

Our families are often our pillar of support while dealing with adverse situations in life. Look at the list of traits and circle the ones that you would associate with your family, and then discuss these questions in class.

respect	gratitude	care	cooperation	guidance	honesty
commitment	humility	generosity	simplicity	loyalty	trust
	oneness	faith	love	affection	

- What are the three most important traits that make a family?
- How are these qualities highlighted in family life?
- Why are these traits important?

HC **Feelings:** Contribution in others' lives – siblings

Reading

Do you have an older sibling who always tells you what to do? Read this story about two brothers who live away from home to attend school. Read on to find out how their relationship changes over time.

My big brother was five years older than me but only three grades ahead. He had begun his studies at the same age as I had, but he didn't like the idea of moving hastily in an important matter like education. He took two years to do one year's work; sometimes he even took three.[1]

I was nine, he was fourteen. He had full right by seniority to supervise me. And I was expected to accept every order of his. He was very studious by nature. He was always sitting with a book open. And perhaps to rest his brain, he would sometimes draw pictures of birds, dogs and cats in the margins of his notebook. Sometimes he would write a name, a word or a sentence ten or twenty times. He would copy a stanza several times in beautiful letters or create new words that made no sense.

I didn't really like studying. To pick up a book and sit with it for an hour was too much of an effort. As soon as I got a chance, I would leave the hostel and go to the playground and play marbles or fly kites or just meet a friend – what could be more fun? But as soon as I came back into the room and saw my brother's **scowling** face, I would be terrified.

His first question would be, 'Where were you?' Always the same question, which he asked in the same tone, and I could only answer with silence. I don't know why I couldn't say that I had just been playing outside.

My silence was an **acknowledgement** of guilt and my brother would always say angrily, 'If you study English this way, you'll be studying your whole life and you won't get one word right! Studying English is no laughing matter. You have to wear out your eyes morning and night and use every ounce of energy. And even then you'll just have a **smattering** of it.

Can't you learn from looking at me? You have seen with your own eyes how hard I work. No matter how many shows and fairs there are, have you ever seen me attend them? Every day there are cricket and hockey matches, but I don't go near them. Despite studying all the time, it takes me two years, or even three, to get through one grade. How do you expect to pass when you waste your time like this? Why waste our father's hard-earned money?'

After such a **dressing-down**, I would start crying. My brother was an expert in the art of giving advice. He'd say such cruel words, **overwhelm** me with such good advice that my spirits would sink, my courage disappear. I would think, 'Why

Literary term

1. This is an example of **irony**. The boy thought that his brother took more time to complete each class because he was studious. But it actually means that he failed the examinations.

scowling: frowning with anger

acknowledgement: acceptance

smattering: incomplete understanding of a subject

dressing-down: scolding

overwhelm: have a strong emotional effect

What did the elder brother do to rest his brain?

miscellaneous: consisting of different kinds of things

expanse: a wide and open area

balmy: pleasantly warm

stratagems: plans to defeat an opponent

ego: a person's sense of self-importance

What was absent in the narrator's timetable?

don't I run away from school and go back home? Why should I spoil my life fiddling with work that's beyond my capacity?'

But after an hour or two, I would get over my despair and resolve to study with all my might. I'd draw up a schedule on the spot. In my timetable, the time for play was entirely absent. Get up at the crack of dawn, wash my hands and face at six, eat a snack, sit down and study. From six to eight, English; eight to nine, arithmetic; nine to nine-thirty, history; then mealtime and afterwards, off to school. A half hour's rest at three-thirty when I got back from school; geography from four to five; grammar from five to six, then a half hour's walk in front of the hostel; six-thirty to seven, English composition; then dinner; translation from eight to nine, Hindi from nine to ten; from ten to eleven, **miscellaneous**; then to bed.

But it's one thing to draw up a schedule, another to follow it. It began to be neglected from the very first day. The inviting green **expanse** of the playground, the **balmy** winds, the commotion on the football field, the exciting **stratagems** of prisoner's base, the speed and flurries of volleyball would all draw me mysteriously and irresistibly.

As soon as I was there, I forgot everything: the life-destroying schedule, the books that strained your eyes – I couldn't remember them at all. And then my brother would start on me again. I would stay well out of his way, try to keep out of his sight, come into the room on tiptoe so he wouldn't know. But if he spotted me, it would be my death.

The yearly exams came round: my brother failed. I passed and was first in my class. There was only two years' difference left between him and me. Now I could be a little proud of myself and my **ego** was inflated. My brother's sway over me was over. As I began to take part freely in the games, my spirits were running high. One day when I had spent the whole morning playing *gilli danda* and came back exactly at mealtime, he said, with all the air of pulling out a sword to rush at me: 'I see you have passed this year and you're first in your class, and you think you've conquered the world. But even great men live to regret their pride, and who are you compared to them? You must have read about Ravan. He was master of the Earth. All the kings of the Earth paid taxes to him. The gods were his servants. But what happened to him in the end? Pride completely finished him, destroying even his name. You've just been promoted one grade and your head's turned by it.

Just passing an exam is not enough, the real thing is to develop your mind. Wait till you reach my class. Algebra and geometry will drive you mad, and God help you with British history! Those poor fellows didn't have names enough to go around. There are scores of Charles! After every name, they have to put second, third, fourth and fifth. If anybody had asked me, I could have reeled off thousands of names. And as for geometry, if you write 'a c b' instead of 'a b c', your whole answer is marked wrong.

They will say, 'Write an essay on punctuality no less than four pages long.' Who doesn't know that punctuality's a very good thing! A man's life is organized according to it, others love him for it and his business prospers from it. Do I need four pages for what I can describe in one sentence! It's not **economising** time, it's wasting it. We want a man to say what he has to say quickly and then to move on.

When you get into my class, you'll find out what's what. Just because you got a first division this time, you're all puffed up. I failed, but I'm still older than you, and I have more experience of the world. Take my advice or you'll be sorry.'

economising: saving

sermons: lectures

Did You Know? History

Charles was the name of two British kings, Charles I and his son, Charles II. Both of them reigned in the seventeenth century.

What really scared the narrator?

It was almost time for school or I don't know when the **sermons** would have ended. I didn't have much appetite that day. If I got a scolding like this when I passed, maybe if I had failed, I would have had to pay with my life. My brother's terrible description of studying in the ninth grade really scared me. I'm surprised I didn't run away from school and go home.

Still, I didn't miss a chance to play. I did study, but much less. Well, just enough to complete the day's work and not be disgraced in class. But the confidence I had gained in myself disappeared and I began to live like a thief.

Then, it was time for the yearly exams again. Once more, I passed and my brother failed. I hadn't done much work; but somehow or the other, I was in the first division. I was astonished too. My brother had just about killed himself with work, memorising every word in the course, studying till ten at night and starting again at four in the morning, and from six until nine-thirty before going to school.

When he heard the results, he broke down and cried. So did I. My pleasure in passing was cut by half. There was only one grade left between my brother and me. The evil thought crossed my mind that if he failed just once more, I'd be at the same level as him. Then what grounds would he have for lecturing me? But I violently rejected the thought. After all, he'd scolded me only with the intention of helping me. Maybe it was because of his advice that I'd passed so easily and with such good marks.

But now, a change came over my brother. He became much gentler. Perhaps he felt that he no longer had the right to tell me off – or at least not as much as before. My independence grew.

I began to take unfair advantage of his **tolerance**. I half started to imagine that I'd pass the next time whether I studied or not. The little I used to study because of my brother ceased too. I found a new pleasure in flying kites and I spent all my time at the sport.

In preparation for a kite tournament, I busied myself in solving problems like how to apply the paste mixed with ground glass on it, to cut the other fellows' kites off their strings.

One day, far from the hostel, I was running along madly to grab hold of a kite. A whole army of boys came racing out to welcome it with long, thick bamboo rods. Nobody cared who was in front or behind them. Suddenly, I **collided** with my brother, who was probably coming back from the market.

He grabbed my hand and said angrily, 'Aren't you ashamed of running with these **ragamuffins** after a one-paisa kite? Have you forgotten that you're not in a junior class anymore? You're in the eighth now, one class behind me. You're smart, there's no doubt about that, but what use is it if it destroys your self-respect? You must have thought, "I'm just a grade behind my brother, so now he doesn't have the right to say anything to me." But you're mistaken. I'm five years older than you and even if you come into my grade, you can never equal the experience I have of life and the world, even if you get an M.A. and a D.Litt. or even a Ph.D.'

'Understanding doesn't come from reading books. Mother never passed any grade and Father probably never went beyond the fifth, but even if we had the wisdom of the whole world, Mother and Father would always have the right to correct us. Maybe they don't know what kind of government they have in America or how many **constellations** there are in the sky, but there are a thousand things they know better than you and me. God forbid, but if I should fall sick today, then you'd be at your wit's end. You wouldn't be able to think of anything except sending a telegram to Father. But in your place, he wouldn't send anybody a telegram or get upset or be worried. He'd find out about the disease himself and try the remedy; then if it didn't work, he'd call some doctor. But you and I don't even know how to make our allowance last through the month. Don't be so proud of almost catching up with me and being independent now. I'll see that you don't go off track. If need be (he held up his fist), I can use this too.'

I was thoroughly shamed by his new approach. I had truly come to know my own insignificance and a new respect for my brother was born in my heart. With tears in my eyes, I said, 'No, no, what you say is completely true and you have the right to say it.' My brother embraced me and

tolerance: willingness to accept something you may not agree with

collided: crashed into (someone)

ragamuffins: dirty, ragged children

constellations: groups of stars that form shapes and have names

What did the narrator spend all his time at?

Did You Know? G.K.

M.A. (Master of Arts), D.Litt. (Doctor of Literature) and Ph.D (Doctor of Philosophy, a research degree) are educational qualifications given by universities after someone completes an advanced level of study.

said, 'I don't forbid you to fly kites. I like it too. But what can I do? If I go off track, how will I watch out for you?'

Just then, a kite that had been cut loose passed over us with its string dangling. A crowd of boys were chasing after it. My brother was very tall. He leaped, caught hold of the string and ran at top speed towards the hostel.

I followed, running close behind him.

Who was chasing after the kite that had been cut loose?

About the author

Dhanpat Rai Srivastav (1880–1936), better known as Munshi Premchand, wrote nearly 250 short stories in Hindi. His works dealt with social issues, including education, the dowry system, widow remarriage and the exploitation of the poor. His best-known novels are *Rangmanch*, *Nirmala* and *Godan*.

Comprehension

Quick Recap

A. Answer the questions in a few lines.

1. Where did the narrator and his brother live? How old were they?
2. Why was there a difference in their age and the number of years by which the elder brother was ahead of the narrator in school?
3. Why did the elder brother remind his sibling about Ravan?
4. What did he say about the difficulties of studying British history and geometry?
5. How did he prepare for the ninth grade exams?
6. Why did both the brothers cry when the elder failed again?
7. Why did the younger brother do well in the exams with little work, while his sibling failed in spite of working hard?

B. Answer the questions with reference to context.

1. *My silence was an acknowledgement of guilt...*
   a. What was the narrator guilty of? Why was he silent?
   b. Which words of his brother made him feel guilty?
   c. What did his brother go on to say while scolding him?
2. *But it's one thing to draw up a schedule, another to follow it.*
   a. What kind of schedule had the narrator drawn up and on whose asking?
   b. Why was it hard for the narrator to follow the schedule? What were the main distractions for him?

c. What thoughts went through the narrator's mind before he decided to draw up the schedule?

d. Was the narrator able to follow it? Why/Why not?

3. *'Understanding doesn't come from reading books...'*

   a. What prompted the elder brother to make such a comment?

   b. Explain the quoted line. How did it apply to the boys' parents?

   c. What did the elder brother say about his role in the narrator's life?

   d. What was the narrator's reaction to his elder brother's words?

Life Skills and Values relationship between siblings, self-worth

Think and answer.

1. Was the elder brother jealous of, or overprotective about his sibling? Give reasons for your answer.
2. Explain the narrator's feelings of surprise, happiness and the 'evil' thought that crossed his mind when he passed the exams and his brother failed yet again.
3. The humour in the story arises from the irony that neither of the two brothers understands their abilities. Do you agree? Give reasons for your answer.
4. Comment on the ending of the story. What does the author convey through the elder brother's action?

21ST CENTURY Critical Thinking

Way with Words

Synonyms and Antonyms

A. Underline the correct synonyms of the words in bold.

1. Rajesh gets really **flustered** when the teacher asks him questions in class. (shocked/nervous/upset)
2. The lady wore a gold necklace with a diamond pendant **dangling** in the middle. (hanging/drooping/swinging)
3. The minister had an **inflated** sense of his own importance, believing that the country could not run without him. (swollen/overestimated/puffed up)
4. The officer was **disgraced** in the media after he was caught taking bribes. (insulted/shamed/embarrassed)
5. Napoleon **conquered** large parts of Europe after coming to power. (ruled/overcame/captured)

B. Underline the most suitable antonyms for the words in bold.

1. The elder brother was a **conscientious** pupil. (indifferent/reckless/disobedient)
2. The two brothers shared a **cordial** relationship. (hostile/friendly/aggressive)

3. The young boy faced a **temporary** setback when he failed to do well in his studies. (fixed/permanent/lasting)
4. The elder brother gave him a **severe** scolding. (harsh/sensitive/mild)
5. The young boy was a **fluent** speaker. (confident/inarticulate/talkative)

Grammar in Use

Main and Subordinate Clauses

You know that a **clause** is a group of words that contains a subject and a finite verb.

Read this sentence.

As soon as I was there, **I forgot everything.**

The words in bold can stand on their own. However, the underlined words depend on the rest of the sentence to convey their meaning.

A clause that can stand on its own is called the **main clause** in a sentence or the **principal clause**. A sentence is also a type of main clause.

A clause that depends on the main clause to complete its meaning is called the **subordinate clause**. Such clauses can be identified by the subordinating conjunctions with which they begin.

A. Underline the main clauses and circle the subordinate clauses in these sentences. One is done for you.

1. *The fruit (that is on the plate) is not fresh.*
2. The hand that rocks the cradle rules the world.
3. Margaret did not say why she went to the doctor.
4. I loved the bag which was on sale yesterday.
5. It was sheer coincidence that we met at the fair today.
6. Anil whispered as if he didn't want anyone to listen.
7. Radha slept soundly after she heard the good news.

B. Complete each sentence with an appropriate clause, according to the instructions. State whether it is a main or a subordinate clause.

1. The lady, ________________, is the Headmistress of this school. (use 'who ...')
2. ________________ is the rumour doing the rounds. (begin: 'That ...')
3. Milkha Singh ran ________________. (use 'as if ...')
4. As I had to attend the cricket camp, ________________. (use 'I could not ...')
5. Tony is sure ________________. (use 'that he ...')
6. The party started ________________. (use 'when ...')
7. Do you know the reason ________________? (use 'why ...')
8. If you can bowl a good over, ________________. (use 'our team ...')

Study Skills

Pronounce Well

This table mentions five common ways of pronouncing the letters ou in a word. Write the words in the box in the appropriate columns according to the pronunciation of ou.

should	mountain	your	soul	would	course	counter	cousin
though	country	thousand	pour	shoulder	young	could	

Rhymes with 'out'	Rhymes with 'roar'	Rhymes with 'good'	Rhymes with 'cup'	Rhymes with 'rose'

Listening and Speaking

Listen to a conversation between two brothers about a school bully. Then, in pairs, enact another conversation on this situation:

You want to go on an overnight excursion with your classmates, but your parents are reluctant to give you permission. Ask your elder sister to help you convince them.

You can use some of these phrases:

- Would you mind ...
- Can you talk to Mother and Father ...
- Please help me get permission ...
- No one else can help me in this matter ...

HC **Recognising feelings and values:** cooperation

Pen it Down

Which, do you think, is better – having a sibling to share things and quarrel with or being the only child who is the centre of the family's attention? Write an essay, arguing either in favour of or against the idea. You can write about these points:

For

- undivided love and attention of parents and relatives
- not expected to live up to the standards of older siblings

Against

- feeling lonely and also facing the chances of being spoilt
- too many expectations from an only child, causing anxiety and low self-esteem

Self Assessment

Now I can

- explore the relationship between two brothers, and understand the meaning of education.
- use synonyms and antonyms, and identify main and subordinate clauses.
- practise the different pronunciations of *ou*, enact a conversation and write an argumentative essay.

Read More

Pride and Prejudice: This novel by Jane Austen explores the lives and fortunes of the five Bennet sisters. Jane, the eldest sibling, and the outspoken Elizabeth share a special bond as they stand by each other through thick and thin.

A Winter's Night: This story by Munshi Premchand is about a farmer, Halku, who stays outside on a bitterly cold night to guard his crops from wild animals. It describes a poor Indian farmer's struggle for survival.

10

The Rime of the Ancient Mariner

Samuel Taylor Coleridge

Let's Get Started

Read the descriptions of these famous literary characters who went on eventful voyages, and fill in their names. Use the help box.

Phileas Fogg	Tintin	Alice
Captain Nemo	Robinson Crusoe	

Character	Name
1. A castaway who spends 28 years on a remote tropical desert island near Venezuela, and encounters cannibals, captives, and rebel sailors, before ultimately being rescued.	
2. A scientific visionary, he roams the depths of the seas in his submarine, the *Nautilus*, assembled from parts manufactured in several different countries. He shares his name with a famous fish from an animated film.	
3. He makes a wager of £20,000 stating he can circumnavigate the world in 80 days or less, and then sets off on a series of exciting adventures, along with his French servant.	
4. She wanders away from a picnic, falls down a rabbit hole, and is whisked away to a fantasy land where things keep getting stranger.	
5. He is a young reporter and adventurer who travels around the world with his dog Snowy, solving crimes along the way.	

Can you name the books or series these characters feature in?

HC **Learning and Awareness:** Evaluating our assumptions and preconditions about life and situations around us

Reading

This is Part I of 'The Rime of the Ancient Mariner', a seven-part poem about a sailor who narrates a strange story to a guest at a wedding and holds him spellbound.

It is an ancient Mariner,
And he stoppeth one of three.
'By thy long grey beard and **glittering** eye,
Now **wherefore** stopp'st thou me?

The Bridegroom's doors are opened wide,
And I am next of kin;
The guests are met, the feast is set:
May'st hear the merry **din**.'

He holds him with his skinny hand,
'There was a ship,' quoth he.
'Hold off! unhand me, grey-beard loon!'
Eftsoons his hand dropt he.

He holds him with his glittering eye—
The Wedding-Guest stood still,
And listens like a three years' child:
The Mariner hath his will.

The Wedding-Guest sat on a stone:
He cannot choose but hear;
And thus spake on that ancient man,
The bright-eyed Mariner.

'The ship was cheered, the harbour cleared,
Merrily did we drop
Below the **kirk**, below the hill,
Below the lighthouse top.

The Sun came up upon the left,
Out of the sea came he!
And he shone bright, and on the right
Went down into the sea.

Higher and higher every day,
Till over the mast at noon—'
The Wedding-Guest here beat his breast,
For he heard the loud **bassoon**.

glittering: sparkling
wherefore: why
din: harsh noise
eftsoons: (here) immediately
kirk: church
bassoon: a stringed musical instrument

Why was the wedding guest in a hurry?

The bride hath paced into the hall,
Red as a rose is she;
Nodding their heads before her goes
The merry **minstrelsy**.

The Wedding-Guest he beat his breast,
Yet he cannot choose but hear;
And thus spake on that ancient man,
The bright-eyed Mariner.

'And now the STORM-BLAST came, and he
Was **tyrannous** and strong:[1]
He struck with his o'ertaking wings,
And chased us south along.

With sloping masts and dipping **prow**,
As who pursued with yell and blow
Still treads the shadow of his foe,
And forward bends his head,
The ship drove fast, loud roared the blast,
And southward aye we fled.

And now there came both mist and snow,
And it grew wondrous cold:
And ice, mast-high, came floating by,
As green as emerald.[2]

And through the drifts the snowy clifts
Did send a **dismal sheen**:
Nor shapes of men nor beasts we **ken**—
The ice was all between.

The ice was here, the ice was there,
The ice was all around:
It cracked and growled, and roared and howled,
Like noises in a **swound**!

At length did cross an Albatross,
Thorough the fog it came;
As if it had been a Christian soul,
We hailed it in God's name.

It ate the food it ne'er had eat,
And round and round it flew.
The ice did split with a thunder-fit;
The helmsman steered us through!

minstrelsy: minstrels (musicians) who would sing, dance and entertain

tyrannous: using power cruelly and unjustly

prow: the pointed front part of a ship

dismal sheen: dull colour

ken: (here) know, understand

swound: an old word for the act of fainting

thorough: (here) old spelling of 'through'

In which direction did the storm blow the ship?

Literary terms

1. This is an example of **personification**. The storm is being imagined as a cruel and powerful person.
2. This is a **simile**. The colour of the icebergs is being compared with the green colour of emeralds.

Did You Know? G.K.

The albatross is the largest sea bird found in the southern Pacific and Antarctic regions. The grey-headed albatross can complete a full circle around the Earth in just over a month.

And a good south wind sprung up behind;
The Albatross did follow,
And every day, for food or play,
Came to the mariner's **hollo**!

In mist or cloud, on mast or **shroud**,
It perched for **vespers** nine;
Whiles all the night, through fog-smoke white,
Glimmered the white Moon-shine.'

'God save thee, ancient Mariner!
From the **fiends**, that plague thee thus!—
Why look'st thou so?'—With my cross-bow
I shot the ALBATROSS.

hollo: (here) the cry to call the bird

shroud: a rope or chain that controls the angle at which a sail is attached in a ship

vespers: evenings

fiends: devils

About the poet

Samuel Taylor Coleridge (1772–1834) started the Romantic movement in English poetry along with William Wordsworth. Coleridge laid great importance on memory and the power of imagination in understanding the world around us. His best-known poems are 'Frost at Midnight' and 'Kubla Khan'.

Comprehension

Quick Recap

A. Answer the questions in a few lines.

1. Why is the mariner described as 'ancient'? Describe two of his physical features.
2. Where did the wedding guest sit to listen to the mariner? Where was he hurrying before he sat down?
3. What happened in the wedding hall after the bassoon sounded?
4. What are the different parts of the ship that have been mentioned in the poem?
5. What does the phrase 'beat his breast' mean? Why did the wedding guest do so?
6. Find examples of repetition in the poem and explain the effects they create.
7. For how many evenings did the albatross perch on the ship? How was it killed?

B. Answer the questions with reference to context.

1. *He holds him with his glittering eye,/The Wedding-Guest stood still,*
   a. How did the mariner detain the guest?
   b. What effect did the mariner's eyes have on the guest?
   c. How had the wedding guest reacted at first to the mariner?
   d. Why did the mariner stop the wedding guest?
2. *And now the STORM-BLAST came, and he/Was tyrannous and strong;*
   He struck with his o'ertaking wings,/And chased us south along.
   a. Who is the speaker in these lines? Who is he speaking to?
   b. How had the voyage been progressing before the storm?
   c. How did the storm affect the ship? Explain the simile used to describe the ship's movement in the storm.
   d. Describe the place where the ship was driven to by the storm.
3. *It ate the food it ne'er had eat,/And round and round it flew.*
   a. What is being referred to as 'it'? What kind of bond did it develop with the crew of the ship?
   b. What effect did its arrival seem to have on the crew?
   c. What is 'it' compared to? What did 'it' do?
   d. What was the wedding guest's response to the speaker's description? Why did he respond in this manner?

Life Skills and Values appreciating Nature in its various forms

Think and answer.

1. How is Nature depicted in the poem? Give examples to support your answer.
2. Why do you think the mariner was so eager to tell his story?
3. Why do you think the mariner shot the albatross?

21ST CENTURY Critical Thinking

Way with Words

USING SAY AND TELL

The poem uses the words **quoth** and **spake** as synonyms of **said**. The words **say** and **tell** are similar in meaning, but different in usage.

We use **say** in direct speech. It is often followed by **to**.
Example: 'Good afternoon,' **said** the teacher **to** the class.

We use **tell** when the purpose is to instruct or inform. It is never followed by **to**.
Example: Have they **told** you anything yet?

A. Complete the sentences with the correct forms of say or tell. Add to if required.

1. The ancient mariner was ____________ an interesting tale.
2. The wedding guest ____________, 'I am in a hurry.'
3. I think you should ____________ him what you really think about the matter.
4. I am terrible at ____________ people what I really think of them.
5. They ____________ a crime never goes unpunished.
6. Sarah ____________ Seema, 'We have extra biology classes tomorrow.'

ARCHAISMS

Archaisms are old-fashioned words or sayings. They are used in literature to create the atmosphere of a distant past.

Look at these lines from the poem.

It is an ancient Mariner,
And he **stoppeth** one of three.
'By **thy** long grey beard and glittering eye,
Now **wherefore stopp'st thou** me?'

The lines can be rewritten in modern English as:

It is an ancient Mariner,
And he **stops** one of three.
'By **your** long grey beard and glittering eye,
Now **why do you stop** me?'

B. Underline the archaic words used in these lines from the poem. Rewrite them by replacing the archaisms with their modern equivalents.

1. 'There was a ship,' quoth he.
2. 'Hold off! unhand me, grey-beard loon!'
3. At length did cross an Albatross,
4. Nor shapes of men nor beasts we ken—
5. Eftsoons his hand dropt he.
6. Thorough the fog it came;

Grammar in Use

TYPES OF SUBORDINATE CLAUSES

You have learned that there are three kinds of subordinate clauses.

An **adjective clause** acts as an adjective in the sentence. It modifies the noun and begins with *who, whose, whom, which* or *that*.

Example: The woman **who came to the library with me** has left. (The clause 'who came to the library with me' modifies the noun **woman**.)

An **adverb clause** modifies the verb in the sentence, answering the questions *where*, *why* and *how much*. It begins with words like *although*, *because*, *after* and *if*.

Example: Father left the firecrackers **where nobody could find them**. (The clause 'where nobody could find them' modifies the verb **left**.)

A **noun clause** functions as a noun and answers the question *what* in a sentence. It acts as the subject, object or complement of the verb and is introduced by words like *who*, *whom*, *whose*, *which* and *that*.

Example: **Who is going to win the prize** is a mystery. (The clause 'who is going to win the prize' answers the question 'What is a mystery?')

A. Match the main clauses in column A with the subordinate clauses in column B. Identify the types of subordinate clauses.

A	B
1. She was the one	a. if we win the bid for it.
2. The school closed down	b. where I left my bag.
3. I remember	c. is an excellent writer.
4. They erected the memorial	d. how to cook a basic meal for yourself.
5. You should know	e. who came to meet me yesterday.
6. We can host the tournament this year	f. where the accident took place.
7. Whoever wrote this letter	g. because it ran out of funds.
8. Harry told his sister	h. when he came out of his room.
9. Tom chased Jerry	i. that he has a secret.

Complex Sentences

Sentences with one independent or main clause and one or more subordinate clauses are called **complex sentences**.

Example: The wedding guest beat his breast **because** he heard the loud bassoon.

Main and the subordinate clauses are joined using subordinating conjunctions like *as*, *although*, *because*, *when*, *whereas*, *unless* or relative pronouns like *who*, *which*, *whose*, *whom* and *that*.

Examples: The wedding guest listened to the mariner. He was getting late for the ceremony.
Although the wedding guest was getting late for the ceremony, he listened to the mariner.
The albatross joined the sailors. They broke through the ice around them.
The sailors broke through the ice around them **when** the albatross joined them.

B. Join the sentences to make complex sentences. Use suitable linkers and make changes as necessary.

1. The students were angry. Their demands had not been met.
2. He thought he had kept the keys. The police would not find them.
3. The bag is trendy. It has been designed by the new company.
4. We anticipated it. The show turned out to be a huge success.
5. The consignment arrived. The shop had shut for the day.
6. India can progress. Her citizens have to strive harder.
7. James took the last wicket. The match was won.
8. A man is standing outside the class. He is a famous photographer.
9. They would arrive late. We knew it beforehand.

Study Skills

Use Your Dictionary

You know that words occur alphabetically in a dictionary. A **guide word** is a word or term that appears at the top of each page or column in a dictionary. The guide word on the left indicates the first entry on the page while the guide word on the right indicates the last entry on it.

A. If the guide words on a page in a dictionary are late and laughter, underline the words from the following list that would occur on the page.

late	latecomer	latch	lather	laughingly
launch	latter	latitude	laudable	latent
last	lash	lateral	lattice	lavender

B. From the remaining words in the list above, find the following.

1. words that would appear on the previous page (before 'late')
2. words that would appear on the next page (after 'laughter')

Listening and Speaking

You have studied about **foot** and **metre** in poetry in the chapter 'Ozymandias'. You know that an **iamb** is a two-syllable foot consisting of an unstressed syllable followed by a stressed syllable.

In 'The Rime of the Ancient Mariner', each stanza has four lines. The first and third lines are in **iambic tetrameter**. This means that the line is made up of four feet, each feet having an unstressed and a stressed syllable. The second and fourth lines are in **iambic trimeter** (each line has three feet). Note, however, that there are instances where the metre does not uniformly follow this pattern.

A. Look at the first stanza, which has been scanned. The stressed syllables are marked with an apostrophe. Each foot is separated by a stroke (/). Count and write down the number of feet in each line.

It -is'/ an -an'/cient- Ma'/ri-ner',
And- he -stop'/peth- one' /of- three'.
'By -thy'/ long- grey'/ beard'- and/ glit'-te/ring- eye',
Now- where'/fore- stopp'st'/ thou- me'?'

B. Now, listen to the following stanzas from the poem and scan them. Separate the syllables using a hyphen, and mark the feet with a stroke (/). Mark the stressed syllables with an apostrophe.

The bridegroom's doors are opened wide,
And I am next of kin;
The guests are met, the feast is set:
May'st hear the merry din.

He holds him with his skinny hand,
'There was a ship,' quoth he.
'Hold off! unhand me, grey-beard loon!'
Eftsoons his hand dropt he.

Pen it Down

The poem ends with the albatross being shot down by the mariner, seemingly without any reason. How do you think the poem ends? Did the mariner have to pay for his act?

Write an account of what you think happened next. Give a suitable title to your story.

You can use these hints: crew horrified – the mariner unable to explain his actions – many tragedies on the voyage – mariner feels guilty – confesses – is forgiven

Self Assessment

Now I can

- read a poem about the mysterious tale of an old man's confession of an unusual crime.
- study the use of literary devices, such as archaisms, similes and personification in the poem.
- use the three types of subordinate clauses, and form complex sentences.
- scan a poem, and write the ending of a story.

Read More

Gunga Din: This poem by Rudyard Kipling is about an Indian water bearer, Gunga Din, who served soldiers in the British army during the Raj. He was found to be more gallant and noble than some of the soldiers who ordered him about.

Listeners: This poem by Walter de la Mare is about a traveller on horseback, who knocks on the door of a cottage. Although it is uninhabited, he has a strange feeling that he is being heard.

11 The Six Napoleons

Sir Arthur Conan Doyle

Let's Get Started

You have read mystery stories featuring different detectives, with their own methods of detection. Look at this character-trait chart and create your own detective. You can also add your own special traits.

male/female old/young/child/ middle-aged	risk-taker/master of disguises/good judge of character/fighter
foreign national/ reporter/old widow/ retired serviceman/ adventurer/solves crimes as a hobby	traditional methods/ powers of observation/ knowledge of society and community/has an assistant and a network of spies

Now think and create a title for a mystery story that would feature your detective.

____

HC **Learning and Awareness:** Understanding what knowledge entails

Reading

Do you enjoy reading detective stories? Have you read the Sherlock Holmes stories? In this story, the ace detective solves the mystery of a set of destroyed statues of Napoleon.

queer: unusual, strange

plaster bust: a plaster of Paris sculpture of a person's head, shoulders and chest

traced: found

relics: objects related to an important person, such as clothing and things they owned

surgery: (here) private clinic

Did You Know? G.K.

Scotland Yard is the headquarters of the London police. Its original location had a back entrance onto a street called Great Scotland Yard. Later, the office was shifted but the name has remained.

What was being destroyed repeatedly?

It was not unusual for Mr Lestrade of Scotland Yard to look in upon us on an occasional evening. On one such occasion, he confessed that he was quite confused by a case he was handling. 'It seems unimportant, but **queer**. Very queer. The first case of burglary was four days ago in the shop of Morse Hudson in Kennington Road. He sells pictures and statues. The shop was left unattended by the assistant for a second. He heard a crash and hurried back to find a **plaster bust** of Napoleon lying in fragments. Although the incident was reported to the policeman on the beat, the hooligan was not **traced**. The second case was more serious and occurred last night.

Dr Barnicot is a great admirer of Napoleon and his house is full of books, pictures and **relics** of the French emperor. He bought two busts of Napoleon from Morse Hudson's shop. These were exact duplicates of the one found broken in the shop. He placed one of them in his house and the other on the mantelpiece of his **surgery** at Lower Brixton. Dr Barnicot came down this morning to find his house burgled during the night. But nothing was missing except the head of Napoleon. It was found, smashed to pieces, in the garden.'

'This is certainly very unusual,' Holmes remarked.

'That is not all. He reached his surgery at noon, and you can imagine his amazement, when he found the window had been opened and broken pieces of the Napoleon were strewn all over the room. It seems to me like the work of some mad man, who hates Napoleon,' Lestrade concluded.

'Without a doubt, this is all very interesting. I would be obliged if you would let me know of any fresh developments in the case.'

Next morning, Holmes informed me that a telegram had come from Lestrade. It said: 'Come instantly, 131 Pitt Street, Kensington—Lestrade.'

We reached the address to find a crowd outside the house. Lestrade led us inside and introduced us to the owner of the house, Mr Horace Harker, a journalist.

'Mr Harker, will you tell us exactly what has occurred?'

'I picked up a bust of Napoleon from Harding Brothers, about four months ago. I often write late into the night or early morning in my room upstairs. It must have been three o'clock. Suddenly, I heard a most horrible scream. I was quite frozen with horror. I seized the **poker** and went down. I entered this room and found the windows open and noticed the bust was gone from the mantelpiece. I walked to the front doorstep and nearly fell over a dead man lying there.'

poker: a long metal rod used for stirring an open fire

trifling: unimportant

by Jove: a British expression that means 'My god!'

expedition: (here) a short trip to get something

'Who was the murdered man?' Holmes asked Lestrade.

'We don't know. He is a tall, sunburnt, strong man, not more than thirty. Poorly dressed. A clasp knife lay in the blood near him. We don't know yet if it was the murder weapon. There is no clue to his identity on his clothes. His pockets contained an apple, a map of London and a photograph. Here it is.'

'What happened to the bust?' Holmes inquired.

What lay near the dead man?

'It has been found in the front garden of an empty house in Campden House Road. It was broken into fragments.'

We accompanied the policeman to Campden House Road. Holmes picked up the broken pieces of the Napoleon and examined them carefully. 'The possession of this **trifling** bust was worth more in the eyes of this strange criminal than a human life,' he observed. 'Let's see now. Why did he choose this house to break the Napoleon? There is another empty house on the street, which he must have passed, before he came to this one.'

'I give up,' said Lestrade.

Holmes pointed to the street lamp above our heads. 'He could see what he was doing here, and he could not there.'

'**By Jove**! That is true,' exclaimed Lestrade.

'And now sir, I think we should pursue our enquiries singly. We can compare notes afterwards. I should like to keep this photograph found in the dead man's pocket, till this evening. Perhaps we could meet at Baker Street at six? I might need your company and assistance for a small **expedition** tonight. Until then, goodbye and good luck.'

We drove down to Morse Hudson, the picture dealer's establishment. Mr Hudson remembered having sold the Napoleons to Dr Barnicot. He told us he had got them from Gelder and Co. in Church Street. Holmes showed him the photograph.

blonde: golden-haired

flushed: reddened

Reading: a town in southern England (pronounced 'redding')

Mafia: a secret organisation of criminals, originally from Sicily in Italy

Who was Beppo?

'Why, it's Beppo!' he cried. 'He was an Italian who made himself useful in the shop and did odd jobs. He left me last week and I have no idea where he went.'

We left the shop to make our way to Gelder and Co. The manager, a big, **blonde** German, answered all of Holmes' questions readily. His books showed that out of a batch of six heads of Napoleon, he had sent three to Morse Hudson and three to Harding Brothers. The bust was made from two profiles of plaster of Paris joined together. This work was usually done by Italians. When Holmes showed him the photograph, his face **flushed** with anger: 'I know this man very well. It was more than a year ago now. He knifed another Italian in the chest and then came here with the police on his heels. Beppo, his name was. He was a good worker too. One of the best. He got off with a year. He must be out by now. We have a cousin of his here. He could tell you where he is.'

'No, no,' Holmes cried, 'not a word to this cousin. The matter is one of great importance. Could you give me the date when Beppo was arrested? I see from your books that the Napoleons were sold on the third of June last year.'

The German looked through his ledger and found that Beppo had received his last wages on the twentieth of May. Holmes thanked him for his cooperation and help, and we made our way to the shop of the Harding Brothers. The owner of the establishment consulted his sales book and informed us that he had sold one Napoleon to Mr Harker, one to Josiah Brown of Laburnum Lodge, Chiswick, and the third to Mr Sandeford of Lower Grove Road, **Reading**. He did not recognise Beppo's photograph but said he had several Italians among his work people. All of them could easily get a peep at his sales book if they wanted to.

Lestrade was already waiting for us when we reached Baker Street. He was jubilant, for he had identified the dead man.

'He is one Pietro Venucci from Naples, who lived in the Italian Quarter. He is connected with the **Mafia** and is one of the greatest cutthroats in London. The other fellow is probably Italian too.'

'But what about the busts?' Holmes asked.

'Never mind the busts, it is the murder we are really investigating. I propose to go to the Italian Quarter and arrest this man on a charge of murder. Will you come with us?'

'I fancy we are more likely to find him in Chiswick tonight. If we don't, I promise to go to the Italian Quarter with you tomorrow. I have an urgent letter to send and then perhaps we should rest a while before we venture out.'

It was eleven o'clock when we drove down to Laburnum Street. We left the cab at a distance from Laburnum Lodge and walked up to the house. The occupants had retired to rest and all was dark, except the light over the hall door. We crouched nearby in the shadow of the fence.

Before long, a **lithe**, dark figure sped up the garden path and vanished past the hall light. A gentle creaking sound told us a window was being opened. Soon we saw the flash of a lantern inside a room. The figure emerged **stealthily** into the patch of light again. He carried something white under his arm. Reassured by the silence, he put the object down and tapped it sharply. In an instant, Holmes had sprung on him and Lestrade and I had him in handcuffs. I saw that he was no other than the man in the photograph.

lithe: (of a person) moving or bending easily, in an elegant way

stealthily: secretively

presume: suppose that something is true

astounded: amazed

But Holmes' attention was not on our prisoner. He was examining the bust of Napoleon the prisoner had stolen out of the house. Just then the door opened and a figure called out: 'Mr Sherlock Holmes? I am Josiah Brown, sir. I got your note and did exactly as you told me. Come in, gentlemen, and have some refreshment.'

But we declined his hospitality, for Lestrade was anxious to get his man into safe quarters.

'I am exceedingly obliged to you, Mr Holmes, but I don't quite understand it all yet,' he confessed. Holmes asked him to come round to Baker Street the next evening, as it was too late for further explanations.

When we met again, Lestrade told us Beppo was a skilful sculptor. He had already been to jail twice, once for a petty theft, and once, as we had already learnt, for stabbing a fellow Italian. He had stubbornly refused to answer any questions about destroying the busts.

We were interrupted by the bell. A gentleman carrying a bag was shown in.

'Mr Sandeford of Reading, I **presume**,' said Holmes.

'Yes sir and I have brought the bust of Napoleon you asked for, with me.'

Holmes placed a ten pound note on the table and asked him to sign a paper in our presence. It simply said that in return for the money, he transferred every possible right to the bust to Sherlock Holmes. Our visitor did so and left.

Holmes then spread a white cloth on the table. He placed the bust on it and struck it a hard blow on the head. The figure broke into pieces. Holmes bent over the shattered remains and then gave a shout of triumph. He held a round dark object in his hand.

'Gentlemen,' he cried, 'here is the famous black pearl of the Borgias.'

Lestrade and I watched him in **astounded** silence.

What did Holmes place on the table?

'You will remember, Lestrade, how this jewel disappeared from the Prince of Colonna's bedroom. It was believed to be stolen by the Italian maid of the Princess. The maid's name was Venucci and I have no doubt, she managed to get it to her brother Pietro, who was in London. Somehow, Beppo got it from him. And while it was in his possession, he was chased by the police. He made for the factory where he worked, and had only a few moments to hide this enormously valuable prize. Six plaster casts of Napoleon were drying there. Beppo made a hole in the wet plaster, dropped in the pearl and covered it once more. No one could possibly find it. But he was sentenced to a year in prison and in the meantime, the six busts were sold off.

Beppo began to search them out. Through a cousin in Gelder and Co., he found out the retail firms who had bought the busts. He found employment with Morse Hudson and tracked down three of them. The pearl was not there. He tracked down the other three busts. The first was at Harker's. There he was **dogged** by Pietro, who held him responsible for the loss of the jewel and he stabbed him in a **scuffle**. Two busts remained. I warned Josiah Brown to avoid a second tragedy. By then I knew what it was that Beppo was after. The name of the murdered man linked one event with the other. Only the Reading bust was left. I bought it in your presence and there it lies.'

'Sir,' said Lestrade at last, 'we are proud of you. And if you would come down to the police station, there is not a man who would not be glad to shake your hand.'

'Thank you,' said Holmes. 'And now Watson, kindly put the pearl in the safe, if you please.'

dogged: followed closely
scuffle: fight

Did You Know? **History**

The Borgias were a politically important and wealthy family in 15th and 16th century Italy. Corrupt and power-hungry, they were suspected of many crimes, especially poisoning.

About the author

Sir Arthur Conan Doyle (1859–1930) was a Scottish author and a trained doctor. His fictional detective Sherlock Holmes is one of the best-loved literary creations of all time. Some of the best books based on Holmes are *The Hound of the Baskervilles* and *A Study in Scarlet*. He also wrote novels about history, spiritualism and his experiences as a doctor.

Comprehension

Quick Recap

A. Number the sentences in the order of the events in the story.

- [ ] Mr Sandeford of Reading brought the bust of Napoleon, which Holmes had asked for.
- [ ] The third bust was found in the front garden of an empty house in Campden House Road, broken into fragments.
- [ ] Holmes found the black pearl of the Borgias in the broken pieces of the last Napoleon bust.
- [ ] Holmes and Lestrade made their way to Gelder and Co.
- [ ] The shop of Morse Hudson in Kennington Road was burgled.
- [ ] Beppo had made a hole in the wet plaster, dropped in the pearl and covered it again.
- [ ] Beppo began to search for the busts once he was released from jail.
- [ ] Dr Barnicot found his house burgled during the night. But nothing was missing except the bust of Napoleon.

B. Answer the questions with reference to context.

1. *On one such occasion, he confessed that he was quite confused by a case he was handling. 'It seems unimportant, but queer. Very queer.'*
   a. Who is being referred to as 'he'? What was the occasion?
   b. What was the first case of burglary that had been reported?
   c. What had been the second case?
   d. What was 'queer' about the cases?
2. *'I entered this room and found the windows open and noticed the bust was gone from the mantelpiece. I walked to the front doorstep and nearly fell over a dead man lying there.'*
   a. Who is the speaker here? How long ago had he bought the bust?
   b. Describe the murdered man. Who did he turn out to be?
   c. What was the murdered man carrying in his pockets?
   d. Where was the bust found?
3. *Before long, a lithe, dark figure sped up the garden path and vanished past the hall light.*
   a. Who was the 'figure'? What do you know of his background?
   b. Where was he? Who else was there at the time?
   c. Why had he come to that place?
   d. What happened immediately afterwards?
4. *Holmes placed a ten pound note on the table and asked him to sign a paper in our presence. It simply said that in return for the money, he transferred every possible right to the bust to Sherlock Holmes.*
   a. Whom did Holmes buy the bust from? Why did he make him sign the agreement?
   b. What did Holmes do next? What startling discovery was made?
   c. Explain in your own words the revelation made by Holmes that solved the case.
   d. What previous crime did Holmes recall to solve the case?

Life Skills and Values cleverness, being observant

Think and answer.

1. Do you think an interesting detective story needs a criminal as clever as the detective? Was Beppo a clever criminal? Give reasons for your answer.
2. What are the elements of a detective story that can be identified from this chapter?
3. How were Sherlock Holmes' methods different from Mr Lestrade's? Give examples from the story.

Way with Words

Words from Detective Fiction

A. These are some words you would find in a detective story. State whether their meanings are true (T) or false (F). Correct the meanings that are wrong.

1. **hunch:** to look carefully at something and note details ☐
2. **perpetrator:** a guilty person ☐
3. **alibi:** a statement or fact used to solve a mystery ☐
4. **sleuth:** another name for a detective ☐
5. **red herring:** a breakthrough that helps you solve a crime ☐
6. **autopsy:** an examination of the vehicles of the suspects ☐

Types of Books

B. Match the type of book in column A with its definition in column B.

A	B
1. atlas	a. a book of information on a subject or instructions for operating a device
2. handbook	b. a collection of maps of the world
3. memoir	c. a collection of poems or short stories by different authors
4. anthology	d. an account written by somebody about their life and experiences
5. encyclopaedia	e. a book of information about the important events of the previous year
6. yearbook	f. a book of synonyms
7. thesaurus	g. a book, often in several volumes, giving information on various subjects in alphabetical order

Grammar in Use

Direct and Indirect Speech

Look at this table which shows the various changes that take place when direct speech is converted to indirect speech.

	Direct Speech	Indirect Speech
Pronouns	*I* *you* *we* *us* *mine* *ours*	*he, she, you* *he, she, me, they/them (if plural)* *they* *them* *his, hers, yours* *theirs*
Tenses	*is/am/are* *was/were* *do* *did* *has/have*	*was/were* *had been* *did* *had done* *had*
Expressions of Time and Place	*now* *today* *yesterday* *tomorrow* *ago* *last night* *here* *next week/month/year* *last week/month/year*	*then* *that day* *the day before* *the following day* *before* *the night before* *there* *the following week/month/year* *the week/month/year before*

You know how to convert a sentence spoken in direct speech to indirect speech and vice versa. We use various kinds of reporting verbs when we convert direct to indirect speech, such as **enquired**, **advised**, **suggested**, **announced**, **complained**, **admitted** and **warned**. Look at the sentences below.

1. 'I am quite confused by a case I am handling,' said Mr Lestrade. (direct)
   Mr Lestrade **confessed** that he was quite confused by a case he was handling. (indirect)
2. 'Mr Harker, will you tell us exactly what has occurred?' Lestrade asked. (direct)
   Lestrade **requested** Mr Harker to tell them exactly what had occurred. (indirect)
3. 'Please come to Baker Street tomorrow evening,' Holmes told him. (direct)
   Holmes **asked** him to come to Baker Street the next evening. (indirect)
4. 'Thank you, Lestrade,' said Holmes. 'Watson, kindly put the pearl in the safe.' (direct)
   Holmes **thanked** Lestrade and requested Watson to put the pearl in the safe. (indirect)

A. Change the following sentences to indirect speech using suitable reporting verbs.

1. 'Are you one of the participants in today's talent show, Renu?' the teacher asked.
2. 'Please come to my office by 9 o'clock tomorrow,' Holmes said to Dr Watson.
3. 'It will be better if you take the local train because traffic is heavy at this time,' Puneet said to Susan.
4. 'Don't cross the river at this point. It is too risky since the bridge is very old. Anything can happen,' the local guide said to the tourists.
5. 'I am guilty as charged. I beg for mercy,' said the man accused of stealing from the bank.
6. 'We have collected evidence. We are ready to arrest the culprits,' the police officer said to the reporters at the press conference.

B. Change the following sentences to direct speech.

1. Next morning, Holmes informed me that a telegram had come from Lestrade.
2. The commander thundered at the recruits to climb faster.
3. Harini pleaded with her mother to let her play for another hour.
4. David Copperfield complained to his uncle that the nurse neglected him completely and favoured his cousin openly.
5. The homeless man was ordered to collect his belongings and leave the building immediately.
6. Farooq suggested that Saroja carry a raincoat, or she would get drenched.

Study Skills

Pronounce Well

Say these words aloud and note the pronunciation of the vowels in bold.

probl**e**m fath**er** circ**u**s th**e** gall**o**p **a**bout

You will notice that the letters in bold, **a**, **e**, **o**, **u**, are all pronounced in the same way in these words. It is a short and weak sound, which rhymes with 'uh' and occurs in the unstressed syllable of the word. This sound is called the **schwa**. It is one of the most common sounds in English.

Circle the letters with the schwa sound in each of these words. Some words may have more than one.

vitamin	occur	carrot	sofa
item	taken	baker	mother
answer	condition	harmony	medium
supply	offence	regiment	refrigerator

Listening and Speaking

A. Listen to an excerpt from Sir Arthur Conan Doyle's novel *The Hound of the Baskervilles* and choose the correct answers.

1. What caused the county people to be sad?
   a. the hound's threat b. Sir Henry's inheritance claim c. Sir Charles' sudden death

2. What kind of a man was Sir Charles Baskerville?
   a. friendly and generous b. bloodthirsty c. unhelpful to the poor
3. Who was Sir Charles' heir?
   a. Dr Mortimer b. Barrymore c. Sir Henry Baskerville
4. Why did Dr Mortimer approach Sherlock Holmes?
   a. because Holmes was famous b. because they were old friends
   c. to solve the hound's mystery
5. Why did Mr Holmes send Dr Watson to Baskerville Hall?
   a. so that Dr Watson could take over b. because Dr Watson was a suspect
   c. to keep track of Sir Henry's activities
6. What did Miss Stapleton ask Watson to do?
   a. to stay away from her brother b. to find Sir Charles' murderer c. to kill the hound

B. State whether the following statements are true (T) or false (F).

1. The man living in a stone hut on the moor was Sir Charles' murderer. ☐
2. Baskerville Hall was in London. ☐
3. Holmes sent Dr Watson to Devonshire. ☐
4. Dr Watson was happy to find Sherlock Holmes on the moor. ☐

Pen it Down

Write a mystery story using the following cues:
a boy and his sister, a vacation, a secret attic, a missing old lady and a parrot

21ST CENTURY Creativity

Self Assessment

Now I can

- understand the way a fictional detective uses logical reasoning to solve crimes.
- identify the key elements of a detective story and learn about certain types of books.
- practise the conversion of sentences from direct to indirect speech and vice versa.
- recognise the *schwa* sound in words and write a mystery story.

Read More

The Westing Game: This book by Ellen Raskin is about the sixteen heirs of the millionaire Sam Westing, who are selected in his will to solve the mystery of his murder.

Trouble in Gangtok: This story, part of the *Feluda* series by Satyajit Ray, is about the way the private detective stumbles upon and solves the case of a business executive's murder while on a vacation in Gangtok.

12

Sport

The Commentator

Gareth Owen

Let's Get Started

There are certain words that are commonly used in English, but they also have specific meanings in the context of football. Read the hints and find six such words in the word grid.

Q	Z	W	B	M	W	E	A	Q	G	R	Y	F	S	D
T	I	Q	O	N	W	V	Y	L	G	C	S	F	C	Y
N	A	B	Y	P	U	D	I	G	Q	I	G	O	A	L
G	W	D	P	S	Y	E	C	O	R	N	E	R	R	N
Z	H	C	W	T	U	F	O	U	L	B	X	W	L	U
W	F	J	P	A	E	E	V	M	E	J	B	A	K	S
T	W	Y	Y	C	B	N	J	V	G	D	S	R	A	C
Q	M	I	S	K	S	C	J	V	S	H	M	D	Y	R
D	P	W	D	L	Q	E	S	E	V	E	R	U	D	W
R	Q	G	G	E	T	C	U	H	G	S	C	U	V	N

1. deal with a problem in a determined or efficient way: T _ _ _ _ _
2. offensive and unpleasant: F _ _ _
3. something that one hopes to achieve: G _ _ _
4. action that is taken to protect someone or something against attack: D _ _ _ _ _ _
5. a point or an area where two or more edges, sides, or surfaces of something join: C _ _ _ _ _
6. a position near the front of something: F _ _ _ _ _ _

Work in pairs and find out what these words stand for in football. Then write the meanings in your notebook.

HC **Feelings:** Participating in neighbourhood/society

Reading

Have you ever played or watched a football match? What did you like the most about it? The commentators make a match come alive with their narration. Read this poem about a young boy who pretends to be playing football for the English national team.

Good afternoon and welcome,
This is Danny Markey your commentator
Welcoming you to this **international**
Between England and Holland,
Which is being played here this afternoon.

At four Florence Terrace.
And the pitch looks in superb condition
As Danny Markey prepares
To **kick off** for England;
And this capacity crowd[1] roars
As Markey, the England captain,
Puts England on the attack.

Straight away it's Markey
With a lovely pass to Keegan,
Keegan back to Markey,
Markey in possession now
Jinking skilfully past the dustbin
And a neat flick inside the cat there,
What a brilliant player this Markey is
And still only nine years old!

Markey to Francis,
Francis to Markey,
Markey is through …
No, he's been **tackled** by the drainpipe;
But he's won the ball back brilliantly
And he's advancing on the Dutch keeper now,
It must be a goal,
He comes off his line
But Markey **chips** him brilliantly
It's a goal
It's gone into Mrs Spence's next door.
And Markey's going round
To ask for his ball back.

international: a match played between two countries

kick off: start the game

jinking, tackled, chips: various football moves

Why did the crowd roar at the beginning of the match?

Literary term

1. This is an example of **alliteration**. The consonant 'c' is repeated in successive words.

dejected: unhappy and disappointed

compost: fertilizer

Did You Know? G.K.

People have played football since ancient times. Balls made of animal parts and linen have even been found in Egyptian tombs. In ancient Rome, it was an Olympic sport, played by as many as fifty-four players. The Chinese sport, *cuju*, was played by the rules of football.

Literary term

2. This is a **hyperbole**. It is only Markey's friends who are cheering for him, not a large crowd of fans.

The crowd is silent now.

If he can't get the ball back
It could be the end of this international.
And now the door's opening
And yes, it's Mrs Spence,
Mrs Spence has come to the door,
And wait a minute, she's shaking her head,
She is shaking her head,
She is not going to let Markey
Have his ball back.

What is the referee going to do?
Markey looks very **dejected** here,
He's walking back, hanging his head.

What's he doing now?
He seems to be waiting
And my goodness me
He's going back,
Markey is going back for the ball,
What a brilliant and exciting move;
He waited until the front door was closed
And then went back for that lost ball.

Why was it important to get the ball back from Mrs Spence?

He's searching now,
He's searching for that ball
Down there by the **compost** heap
And wait a minute,
He's found it!
He's found that ball
And that's marvellous news
For the hundred thousand fans gathered here,[2]
Who are showing their appreciation
In no uncertain fashion.
But wait a minute,
The door's opening once more;
It's her, it's Mrs Spence!
And she is waving her fist
And shouting something
But I can't make out what it is.

She's obviously not pleased.
And Markey's off,
He's running round in circles
Dodging this way and that
With Mrs Spence **in hot pursuit**,
And he's past her,
What skills this boy has.

dodging: moving quickly to one side to avoid somebody

in hot pursuit: chasing someone to catch them

About the poet

Gareth Owen (1936–) has written several plays and poems for children. He often presents commonplace activities in a child's everyday life like a special event. 'Salford Road', 'Song of the City' and *The Man with Eyes Like Windows* are some of his other writings for children.

Comprehension

Quick Recap

A. Explain these lines with reference to context.

1. *And this capacity crowd roars*
2. *No, he's been tackled by the drainpipe;*
3. *What a brilliant and exciting move.*
4. *She's obviously not pleased.*

B. Answer the questions in a few lines.

1. Who introduced himself in the poem as the commentator?
2. Where was the game being played?
3. Which two teams were supposed to be playing against each other? How many 'players' are mentioned by name?
4. How many fans were supposed to have gathered to watch the game?
5. Narrate the opening moments of the game, until Markey runs past the dustbin.
6. Describe how Markey scored his goal.
7. What trouble lay in store for Markey?
8. How did Markey rescue the ball?

Life Skills and Values

imagination, humour, quick-thinking

Think and answer.

1. What are the actual and imagined settings of the poem?
2. What are the humorous elements in the poem?
3. What kind of a boy was Markey?
4. What are the various features of the poem that make it sound like a commentary?

21st Century Critical Thinking

21st Century Flexibility

Way with Words

IDIOMS WITH *TALK*

A. Here are some idiomatic expressions with the word talk. Match the expressions in column A with their meanings in column B.

A	B
1. talk big	a. talk continuously
2. talk nineteen to the dozen	b. talk about one's work during a social occasion, where it is inappropriate
3. talk shop	c. talk about unimportant things
4. talk of the town	d. boast
5. make small talk	e. the centre of attention

WORDS RELATED TO FOOTBALL

B. Unscramble these words related to football and complete the sentences.

1. The newly opened high school has an excellent ________________ for athletic contests, seating twenty-five thousand. (imudast)
2. He was penalised for repeatedly challenging the ________________'s decisions. (senilanm)
3. There were thousands of ________________ (sattropesc) waiting at the gates for the finals to begin.
4. The ________________ (eraodbsocr) showed that only fifteen minutes remained of the match.
5. The ________________ (feereer) for the match was a former footballer from Norway.
6. The young footballer was warned that another display of temper would earn him a severe ________________. (eptlyan)
7. I have never understood the rules for ________________ (ifsdoef), even though it has been explained to me several times.

Grammar in Use

TENSES

You know that tenses refer to present, past and future time. They take four forms: the simple, the continuous, the perfect and the perfect continuous.

The **present participles** are the *-ing* form of verbs. They refer to incomplete actions or states of being. We use the present participles to form the continuous tenses.

Look at these examples.

present continuous	past continuous	future continuous	past perfect continuous	future perfect continuous
Markey **is advancing** on the Dutch keeper now.	Mrs Spence **was shaking** her head.	I **will be visiting** my grandparents tomorrow.	Bailey **had been playing** football in the park all evening.	By 2023, Rohit **will have been studying** physics for two years.

The **past participles** are verb forms that act as adjectives in sentences. They usually end in *-ed*, *-d*, *-t*, *-en* or *-n*. They refer to actions that have been completed in the past but whose effects are still present. We use the past participles to form the perfect tenses.

Look at these examples.

present perfect	past perfect	future perfect
Markey **has brought** the ball back.	Mrs Spence **had been disturbed** by the boys' game.	By 2022, Reza **will have graduated** from college.

A. Complete the sentences with the given form of the verbs.

1. By this time next year, we ______________ all the books we bought at the book fair. (future perfect form of 'read')
2. The train ______________ already ______________ by the time we reached the station. (past perfect form of 'arrive')
3. She ______________ her dance moves all day without taking a break. (present perfect continuous form of 'practise')
4. He ______________ in the lake now. (present continuous form of 'swim')
5. She ______________ in this firm for ten years. (past perfect continuous form of 'work')
6. By 2022, India ______________ fighter jets for the air force locally. (future continuous form of 'manufacture')

B. Complete the passage with the correct form of the given verbs.

All over the world, nowadays there ______________ (be) much debate on the kind of toys children should play with. People now ______________ (believe) that Barbie dolls ______________ (create) an unrealistic image in girls about the way they should look, while video games ______________ (consider) too violent for boys. The best toys are those that ______________ (nurture) children's imagination. There ______________ (be) a time when toys for boys and girls ______________ (be) as different as chalk and cheese. Today, girls often ______________ (play) with action figures, while parents ______________ (encourage) boys to do craft work. This ______________ (instil) an understanding about gender equality in children from a young age. Hopefully, this way, we ______________ (erase) gender differences prevalent in the society.

Study Skills

Use Your Dictionary

A **headword** in a dictionary is the word or phrase whose meaning is given.

It is usually set in bold so that it is easily recognisable. All the meanings of a word are listed under the headword.

Example: man *noun* 1. an adult human male 2. all mankind
verb 1. be in charge of or operate something

Using a dictionary, write these meanings under the correct headwords.

1. go away
2. pleasant
3. move your hand in greeting
4. sugary
5. photograph
6. give something to someone when you die
7. break with a sharp noise
8. confectionary
9. a period of time when you are away from your job
10. something continuing for a long time
11. a moving wall of water on the sea
12. speak impatiently

sweet	leave	snap	wave

Listening and Speaking

Listen to someone apologising to another person. Then, work in pairs to enact the conversation that Markey would have had with Mrs Spence.

Here are some phrases that you can use in your conversation:

Admitting your mistake	Offering an apology
• I take full responsibility ...	• Please accept my sincere apology ...
• I understand that my behaviour is inexcusable ...	• I am terribly sorry ...
• It is my fault, I shouldn't have done that ...	• I promise this will never happen again ...

Pen it Down

A. Your school is organising the annual inter-house mixed cricket match. It is a unique feature of the school, where girls and boys play together on the same team. Make a poster inviting students to the match and cheer their respective houses. Mention the date, time, and venue of the match, and give a suitable heading.

B. Imagine that you played an important role in an exciting match played in your school. Write a paragraph on it, including details about the teams, the most exciting moments of the match and how your actions impacted the outcome.

________________ (heading)

PARTICIPATING HOUSES:

DATE:

TIME:

VENUE:

Self Assessment

Now I can

- read and appreciate a humorous commentary on a game of football.
- understand the two layers of meaning in the poem.
- use words related to football and practise tenses.
- enact a conversation, make a poster and write a paragraph on a topic.

Read More

Conversation Piece: This humorous poem by Gareth Owen is about a teacher questioning a student who is repeatedly late for class, misses tests and won't do what the teacher asks. He cites the death of his grandmother as the reason for all of these.

Playing it My Way—My Autobiography: This is the autobiography of Indian cricketer Sachin Tendulkar, who recounts his life, starting from the first time he picked up the cricket bat as a child.

Research and Write

A. 'The Six Napoleons' is set in Victorian London and refers to various areas and streets in the city.

Look at a current map of London and mark the areas mentioned in the story. Then, research and answer the following questions:

- Which parts of London are the areas and streets located in?
- Do the areas have any defining characteristics? (whether they are noted for particular businesses, are wealthy neighbourhoods, their historical relevance, etc.)
- What features of a city are mentioned in the story that we continue to see in cities today?

B. It is often said that a film can never be as good as the book that inspires it. Do you agree?

Watch any one of the films based on the adventures of Sherlock Holmes, for example, 'The Hound of the Baskervilles' and write about the differences and similarities between the film and the book.

C. The story 'Elder Brother' is told from the point of view of the younger, smarter sibling. How do you think relations between siblings are affected when the younger of the two is more intelligent?

1. **Write an imaginary diary entry by the elder brother, where he talks about his deepest feelings, including his concerns about their changing relationship and his love for his brother.**

HC evaluating our assumptions about relationships

2. **You read about the ways in which learning took place for both the brothers at school. Language learning is necessary to build the vocabulary of students. Observe a 'language week' in class by completing the following tasks assigned for each day of the week. Each task is related to a figure of speech or language structure.**

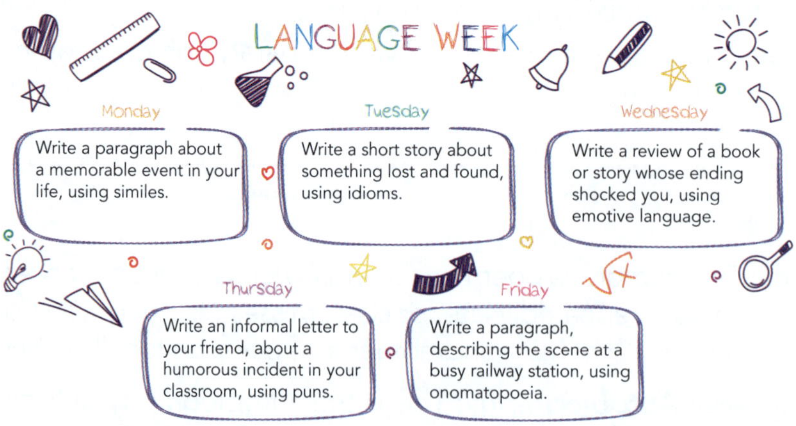

D. In 'The Commentator', the poet describes children playing football in their neighbourhood as an imaginary international match with a large crowd in attendance.

Think of another ordinary, everyday event, such as getting ready for school, studying in class or having an argument with a classmate, and describe it as a sport being watched by an excited audience.

short story

13

Love and Sacrifice

The Gift of the Magi

O. Henry

Let's Get Started

A. Have you read any stories of sacrifice in folk tales or fairy tales? Make a list of any three such stories in the table.

Name of the story and the country of its origin	Who made the sacrifice and for whom	What was sacrificed

B. Have a class discussion on the topic 'Love and sacrifice are outdated foolishness in today's world.'

Take turns to express your views and reasons for it, and the points can be put up on the board. At the end of the discussion, take a vote on which side was more convincing in their arguments.

HC **Recognising feelings and values:** affection and care

Reading

Should gifts be valued for their utility or the thought that goes into them? Read a story about a young couple with little money, who want to buy each other what they most desire for Christmas.

One dollar and eighty-seven cents. That was all. And sixty cents of it was in pennies. Pennies saved one and two at a time by **bulldozing** the grocer and the vegetable man and the butcher until one's cheeks burned with embarrassment. Three times Della counted it. One dollar and eighty-seven cents. And the next day would be Christmas.

bulldozing: using force while dealing with someone

There was nothing left for Della but to flop down on the shabby little couch and howl.

Della and her husband lived in a furnished flat at $8 per week. In the **vestibule** below was a letterbox into which no letter would go and an electric button from which no mortal finger could **coax** a ring. On it was a card bearing the name 'Mr James Dillingham Young'.

vestibule: a room just inside the entrance to a building leading to other rooms or corridors

coax: (here) to work on a device carefully to make it work

flung to the breeze: displayed with pride

unassuming: not arrogant, modest

cascade: (here) resembling a waterfall

faltered: hesitated

Where did Jim and Della live and how much did they pay as rent?

The 'Dillingham' had been **flung to the breeze** during a former period of prosperity when James was being paid $30 per week. Now, when the income was shrunk to $20, the letters of 'Dillingham' looked blurred, as though they were thinking of contracting to an **unassuming** 'D'. But whenever Mr James Dillingham Young came home, he was called 'Jim' and greatly hugged by Mrs James Dillingham Young, introduced to you as Della.

Della finished her cry and attended to her cheeks with the powder rag. She stood by the window and looked out dully at a grey cat walking a grey fence in a grey backyard. Tomorrow would be Christmas and she had only $1.87 with which to buy Jim a present. She had saved every penny she could for months, but twenty dollars a week doesn't go far. Expenses had been greater than she had calculated.

Many a happy hour she had spent planning for something nice for Jim. Something fine and rare—something just a little bit near to being worthy of the honour of being loved by him.

There was a mirror between the windows of the room. Suddenly, she whirled from the window and stood before the glass. Her eyes were shining, but her face had lost its colour. Rapidly, she pulled down her hair and let it fall to its full length.

There were two possessions of the James Dillingham Youngs in which they took a mighty pride. One was Jim's gold watch that had been his father's and his grandfather's. The other was Della's hair.

Della's beautiful hair fell about her, rippling and shining like a **cascade** of brown waters. It reached below her knee. She did it up again nervously. She **faltered** only once and stood still while a tear or two splashed on the worn red carpet.

On went her old brown jacket and old brown hat. With a whirl of skirts and with the sparkle still in her eyes, she cluttered out of the door and down the stairs to the street.

Where she stopped, the sign read, 'Mme Sofronie. Hair Goods of All Kinds.'

'Will you buy my hair?' asked Della.

'I buy hair,' said Madame. 'Take yer hat off and let's have a look at it.'

Whom did Jim's gold watch belong to?

Down rippled the brown cascade.

'Twenty dollars,' said Madame, lifting the mass with a practised hand.

The next two hours tripped by on rosy wings. She was ransacking the stores for Jim's present.

She found it at last. It had been made for Jim and no one else. There was no other like it in any of the stores, and she had turned all of them inside out. It was a platinum **fob chain**, simple and pure in design. Quietness and value—the description applied to both. Twenty-one dollars they took for it and she hurried home with the 87 cents. With that chain on his watch, Jim might be properly anxious about the time in any company. Grand as the watch was, he sometimes looked at it on the sly because of the old leather strap that he used in place of a chain.

When Della reached home, her excitement dimmed a little. She got out her curling irons and lighted the gas and went to work, repairing the **ravages** made by generosity added to love.

Within forty minutes, her head was covered with tiny, close-lying curls that made her look like a **truant** schoolboy. She looked at her reflection in the mirror long, carefully and critically.

At 7 o'clock, the coffee was made and the frying pan was on the back of the stove, ready to cook the chops.

Jim was never late. Della doubled the fob chain in her hand and sat on the corner of the table. Then she heard his step on the stair down on the first flight and she turned white for just a moment. She had a habit of saying little silent prayers about simple everyday things and now she whispered, 'Please, God, make him think I am still pretty.'

The door opened and Jim stepped in and closed it. He looked thin and very serious. Poor fellow, he was only twenty two—and to be burdened with a family! He needed a new overcoat and he was without gloves.

Jim stepped inside the door. His eyes were upon Della and there was an expression in them that she could not read, and it terrified her. It was not anger, surprise, disapproval or horror, any of the sentiments that she had been prepared for. He simply stared at her fixedly with that peculiar expression on his face.

fob chain: a small chain attached to a pocket watch

ravages: damages

truant: a student who stays away from school without permission

trance: a state in which somebody is not aware of what is happening around them

hysterical: in a state of extreme excitement

tortoiseshell: the semi-transparent shell of turtles, once used to make ornaments

dandy: something impressive

Della wriggled off the table and went to him.

'Jim, darling,' she cried, 'don't look at me that way. I sold my hair because I couldn't have lived through Christmas without giving you a present. It'll grow out again. My hair grows awfully fast. Say 'Merry Christmas!' Jim, and let's be happy.'

Jim looked about the room curiously.

'You say your hair is gone?' he said, with an air almost of idiocy.

'You needn't look for it,' said Della. 'It's sold, I tell you. Be good to me, for it went for you.'

Jim quickly awoke out of his **trance**. He embraced his Della. He drew a package from his overcoat pocket and threw it upon the table.

'Don't make any mistake, Dell,' he said, 'I don't think there's anything in the way of a haircut that could make me like my girl any less. But if you'll unwrap that package you'll see why I was surprised at first.'

White and agile fingers tore at the string and paper. There was a delighted scream of joy; and then, a quick change to **hysterical** tears and wails, followed by Jim's soft words of comfort to Della.

For there lay the set of combs that Della had worshipped for long in a shop window. Beautiful combs, pure **tortoiseshell**, with jewelled rims—just the shade for her beautiful vanished hair. They were expensive and her heart had yearned for them without the least hope of possession. And now, they were hers, but the tresses that should have adorned them were gone.

She hugged them to her heart. Then she looked up with dim eyes and a smile and said, 'My hair grows so fast, Jim!'

> What did Della tell Jim as consolation, after seeing her present?

But Jim had not yet seen his beautiful present. She held it out to him eagerly upon her open palm, the dull, precious metal seeming to flash.

'Isn't it a **dandy**, Jim? I hunted all over town to find it. You'll have to look at the time a hundred times a day now. Give me your watch. I want to see how it looks on it.'

Instead of obeying, Jim just smiled.

'Dell,' said he, 'let's put our Christmas presents away and keep 'em a while. They're too nice to use just at present. I sold the watch to get the money to buy your combs.'

The Magi were wise men—wonderfully wise men—who brought gifts to the babe in the manger. They invented the art of giving Christmas presents. This is the uneventful story of two foolish children in a flat who most unwisely sacrificed for each other the greatest treasures of their house. But let it be said that of all who give gifts, these two were the wisest. They were the Magi.

Did You Know? History

According to *The Bible*, the Magi were wise men who came to worship the infant Jesus Christ and brought gifts of gold, frankincense and myrrh.

About the author

O. Henry (1862–1910) was the pen name of the American writer, William Sydney Porter. He was a master of the short-story genre, whose works are characterised by a surprise twist at the end. He was a keen observer of everyday life and most of his characters are ordinary people. Some of his most-loved stories are 'After Twenty Years' and 'A Retrieved Reformation'.

Comprehension

Quick Recap

A. Answer the questions.

1. What were the full names of Jim and Della? What were their prized possessions?
2. Give three examples from the story which suggest that Jim and Della were poor.
3. Explain the metaphor in the phrase 'cascade of brown waters'.
4. Where did Della go to sell her hair? How much did she sell it for? Why did she hesitate before going ahead with her idea to sell her hair?
5. Describe the fob chain. Why did Della feel that the fob chain was the perfect gift for Jim?
6. Why was Della worried that Jim might not find her pretty anymore?
7. What gift had Jim bought for Della? What was her reaction to it?
8. Who were the Magi? What custom did they establish?

B. Answer these questions with reference to context.

1. *One dollar and eighty-seven cents. That was all.*
   a. What did this amount signify?
   b. How had Della saved money to buy Jim a Christmas present?
   c. What had she thought while trying to save money?

2. *'My hair grows awfully fast.'*
   a. Who said these words and to whom?
   b. Why did the speaker say these words? What was the listener's reaction to her altered appearance?
   c. Why did she repeat these words again to the listener?
3. *'Let's put our Christmas presents away and keep 'em a while. They're too nice to use just at present.'*
   a. Who said these words and to whom?
   b. What Christmas present had he received?
   c. Why did he say that their presents were *'too nice to use just at present'*?

Life Skills and Values selflessness, love and sacrifice

Think and answer.

1. Explain the significance of the title of the story. Why do you think Jim and Della are called the 'Magi'?
2. Do you think Jim and Della's actions were foolish? Give reasons for your answer.
3. Make a comparison of the character traits of Jim and Della.

HC Mutuality in feelings in relationships

Way with Words

Idioms Related to Money

A. Look at these idioms and colloquialisms related to money. Write what they mean and make sentences with them.

1. hard up for money
2. have money to burn
3. strapped for cash
4. pay through your nose (for something)
5. to be loaded

Suffixes

B. Add suitable suffixes to the words given in brackets to complete the sentences. You may have to change the form of the words.

1. There should be no _______________ (censor) of the media if we want to encourage free speech in our country.
2. The _______________ (collide) between the car and the lorry shook the entire neighbourhood.

3. ________________ (rest) and ________________ (bore) made him take up an overseas project.
4. There was not enough ________________ (store) space in the new house.
5. Mountaineers must have remarkable powers of ________________ (endure).
6. Good ________________ (govern) must be the aim of every political party.
7. Her most ________________ (admire) quality is her calmness under pressure.
8. The ________________ (courage) soldiers pushed back the invaders from the border.

Grammar in Use

Using For, During and While

Look at these sentences.

She had saved every penny she could **for** months.

The 'Dillingham' had been flung to the breeze **during** a former period of prosperity.

She stood still **while** a tear or two splashed on the worn red carpet.

For, **during** and **while** are used to talk about time. Note the following differences in the usage of the three words.

For denotes the time taken for an action. It is followed by a period of time.

During indicates the connection between parallel events or an event connected to a time period. It is followed by a noun.

While talks about an action taking place simultaneously with another.

A. Complete the sentences using for, during or while.

1. There has been heavy rainfall in the area ________________ some time now.
2. I fell asleep ________________ the concert.
3. Shilpa practised the guitar ________________ her summer vacation.
4. My brother always sings ________________ he is in the shower.
5. I waited ________________ a year after my accident before resuming dancing lessons.
6. I like to listen to music ________________ exercising.
7. It's best to keep quiet ________________ meals.
8. The President's speech was perfect. She must have practised ________________ days.

Question Tags

You know that a positive statement is followed by a negative question tag, while a negative statement is followed by a positive one.

If the sentence has the verb 'to be' or any other auxiliary verb, it is used in the tag.

Example: These people are poor, **aren't they**?

If there is another main verb in the sentence, we use the correct form of 'do' in the tag.

Example: Jim loved Della very much, **didn't he**?

Exception: A sentence beginning with 'I am' is followed by the question tag 'aren't I?'.

B. Add suitable question tags to the following sentences.

1. John and Riya do not like mathematics, ________________
2. Ed will return home tonight, ________________
3. She could have bought a new car with all that money, ________________
4. I am so clever, ________________
5. They aren't coming for the presentation, ________________
6. You like pop music a lot, ________________

Subordinating Conjunctions

You know that complex sentences include a main clause and one or more subordinate clauses.

Subordinating conjunctions join the clauses in complex sentences. Some common subordinating conjunctions are *when, while, before, after, since, as, as soon as, like, where, wherever, because, although, though, even if, even though, if* and *unless.*

Example: **When** Della reached home, her excitement dimmed a little.

In this sentence, the subordinating conjunction **when** connects the main clause, 'Della reached home' with the subordinate clause, 'her excitement dimmed a little'.

C. Join the sentences using the given subordinating conjunctions.

1. Work hard. You will succeed. (if)
2. He better hurry up. He will be late. (unless)
3. Anna is an accomplished singer. She is prone to stage fright. (though)
4. Harsh is going to the UK next year. He wants to complete his higher studies there. (as)
5. We all respect him. He is a helpful person. (because)
6. We had visited the amusement park. The park was shut for lockdown. (before)

Study Skills

Use Your Dictionary

In addition to single words, we can also find the meanings of multi-word entries in a dictionary. These can be phrasal verbs, compound nouns and adjectives, idioms and even figures of speech.

Using your dictionary, find the meanings of these multi-word entries. Then make sentences of your own with any six of them.

1. pull down   2. took for   3. bite the dust

4. honour-bound
5. public speaking
6. well read
7. ill-prepared
8. driving licence
9. big fish in a small pond
10. white lie
11. as blind as a bat
12. step down

Listening and Speaking

Listen to a passage about a group of sisters receiving their Christmas gifts and answer the questions in a few sentences.

1. What did Jo feel when she saw no stockings that Christmas morning?
2. What gifts had the girls received from their mother for Christmas?
3. Where was their mother that morning?
4. What gift had Amy planned to give their mother?
5. Why was Beth anxious about her gift?
6. What did Jo cry out when she heard footsteps in the hall?
7. Who do you think is the eldest of the four sisters?
8. Suggest two adjectives to describe Jo.

Pen it Down

A. Write a review of the story 'The Gift of the Magi'. Give your opinion on its strengths and weaknesses and state your reasons for liking or disliking it.

B. How do you think the story would have ended if Jim and Della had decided on different presents? Write an alternative ending to the story, starting with Jim returning home in the evening.

21ST CENTURY Creativity

Self Assessment

Now I can

- read about selfless love and the value of gifts, and understand who the Magi were.
- understand the difference between *for*, *while* and *during*, practise question tags and join sentences using subordinating conjunctions.
- review a story and write an alternate ending to a story.

Read More

The Last Leaf: This story by O. Henry is about a young girl suffering from pneumonia. She links her survival to the last leaf of a storm-ravaged vine outside her window. Her old neighbour, an unknown artist, takes it upon himself to save her life.

Dusk: This story by Saki is about a man's encounter with a stranger who tells him a story and asks him for money. The man is not convinced, but a twist in the tale works to the stranger's benefit.

14

The Last Wolf

Mary TallMountain

Let's Get Started

The United Nations Sustainable Development Goal 15 talks about sustainably managing forests and halting loss of biodiversity. Man's insatiable greed has led to the loss of habitat and ultimately taken the lives of many different species of animals. Nature helps us survive, and we should also do our bit in saving the flora and fauna around us.

Look at the pictures of some endangered animals and match them with the things they are hunted for.

ivory horns   meat   medicine   jewellery   luxury items

lemur

Sunda pangolin

snow leopard

Sumatran rhino

sea turtle

Active Participation: Exploring maintenance of balance in the animal and human orders

Reading

In the clash between human civilisation and nature, the latter has frequently lost. When you travel through your city, do you wonder whether, centuries ago, it might have been part of a forest and home to many animals? Read this poem about a wolf, the last of its kind, who travels across a modern city to meet someone.

The last wolf hurried toward me
through the ruined city
and I heard his **baying** echoes
down the steep smashed **warrens**
of Montgomery Street and past
the ruby-crowned highrises
left standing
their lighted elevators useless

Passing the flicking red and green
of traffic signals
baying his way eastward
in the mystery of his wild **loping** gait
closer the sounds in the deadly night
through clutter and **rubble** of quiet blocks
I hear his voice ascending the hill
and at last his low whine as he came
floor by empty floor to the room
where I sat
in my narrow bed looking west, waiting
I heard him **snuffle** at the door and
I watched

He trotted across the floor
he laid his long gray **muzzle**
on the spare white spread
and his eyes burned yellow
his small dotted eyebrows quivered

Yes, I said.
I know what they have done.

baying: howling

warrens: a maze of buildings

loping: running with long, relaxed steps

rubble: broken stones and bricks from ruined buildings

snuffle: breathe noisily through the nose

muzzle: the nose and mouth of an animal

What did the wolf do after entering the poet's room?

Did You Know? Science

The howl of each wolf is unique. It is used by wolves in the same pack as well as scientists to identify each animal.

About the poet

Mary TallMountain (1918–1994) was a poet and writer of Native American heritage. Her poems explore the themes of loss of family and homeland. She was very active in the Native American literature movement. Some of her well-known poems include 'Good Grease' and 'Indian Blood'.

Comprehension

Quick Recap

A. Answer the questions in a few lines.

1. Where was the wolf headed? Describe the way the wolf moved as he travelled across the city, referring to the verbs used to describe his walk.
2. Name and explain the figure of speech in the phrase 'ruby-crowned highrises'.
3. Which street does the wolf pass through? Compare and contrast the 'warrens' and 'highrises' the wolf passes.
4. What passing mention does the poet make about the way the wolf looked?
5. What are the various words used to describe the cry of the wolf?
6. What do the wolf's movements and his cries indicate about his state of mind?

B. Answer the questions with reference to context.

1. *Passing the flicking red and green/of traffic signals*
   baying his way eastward/in the mystery of his wild loping gait
   a. Who is being referred to in this extract? Describe the city 'he' passes through.
   b. Why is his gait described as 'mysterious'?
   c. During what time of the day was 'he' travelling? How do you know?
2. *...as he came/floor by empty floor to the room*
   where I sat/in my narrow bed looking west, waiting
   a. Who do you think the speaker is?
   b. What was the speaker waiting for? Why?
   c. Where was the speaker? Describe the room the speaker was in.
3. *...his eyes burned yellow/his small dotted eyebrows quivered*
   Yes, I said./I know what they have done.
   a. Describe the expression in the eyes of the wolf.
   b. Why did the wolf whine as he came to the speaker's room?
   c. Explain the last line of the extract. Why did the speaker say these words?

Life Skills and Values — perils of urbanisation, saving wildlife

Think and answer.

1. What does the sad and empty picture of urban life in the poem stand for?
2. What does the wolf symbolise in the poem? Why do you think he came to the speaker?
3. What is the message of the poem?

HC understanding the purpose of and interconnectedness between the animal and human orders

Way with Words

Contextual Usage

A. Complete the sentences with words from the poem.

1. Tom's lively ____________ as he walked into class suggested that he was pleased about something.
2. The only way up the mountain is by a ____________ climb that is ten kilometres long.
3. If you keep ____________ the switch on and off, it might get damaged.
4. My sister embroidered a ____________ with beautiful floral patterns for her sewing class.
5. The dog's nose ____________ with greed as he smelled the delicious meat.
6. Do you have a ____________ pair of shoes I could borrow? Mine got wet in the rain.

Idioms Related to Wolves

B. Complete the following sentences using these idioms related to wolves. You may have to change the form of some of the words.

wolf in sheep's clothing	cry wolf	keep the wolf from the door
lone wolf	thrown to the wolves	

1. As winter set in and it became more and more difficult to ________________, Harry's father decided to take a job in the city.
2. Kurt is nothing but a ________________. All along, he fooled us into believing that he was our biggest supporter.
3. The businessman pleaded that his debts be cancelled but he was ________________ by the company he had himself founded.
4. His habit of ________________ will get him into trouble some day.
5. As a private detective, Jagdish had always worked as a ________________.

Grammar in Use

JOINING SENTENCES: PARTICIPLES

You know that participles are words that are used as adjectives. They qualify the nouns that follow them.

We use present, past and perfect participles to join sentences.

Look at these sentences.

1. He trotted across the floor/he laid his long gray muzzle/on the spare white spread
   These two sentences can be joined and rewritten as:
   Trotting across the floor, he laid his long gray muzzle on the white spread.

   The word **trotting** is a present participle. It can be used to join two simple sentences whose subject is the same and in which the actions (**trotted** and **laid**) are happening at the same time.
2. He finished his work. He sat down to dinner.
   The sentences can be rewritten as:
   Having finished his work, he sat down to dinner.
   Here, the action of the first sentence is complete before the action in the second. We join such sentences using the structure, *having* + past participle form of the verb.

Join these sentences using participles.

1. She finished her breakfast. She left for the trek. (begin: Having ...)
2. We heard a loud noise. We ran to the window. (begin: Hearing ...)
3. We spent the day. We played cards. (join using the present participle of 'played'.)
4. The thief jumped over the fence. The thief escaped. (begin: Jumping ...)
5. I felt bored. I decided to go for a movie. (begin: Feeling ...)
6. Simon went to bed. He thought about the next day's match. (use present participle of 'thought')
7. Mr Sharma was a forthright person. He always spoke his mind. (begin: Being ...)
8. Madhu walked to school. She was worried about the exam results. (use present participle of 'worried')

Study Skills

Pronounce Well

The letter u has five main pronunciations. In the table given in the next page, write the given words under the word with which it matches in the pronunciation of u.

Then, write two more words of your own in each column.

ruby	muzzle	nurse	useless	pull
snuffle	burned	conclude	duty	bush

run	rule	cute	push	fur

Listening and Speaking

The destruction of wildlife and nature is an unavoidable fallout of development and progress, which we have to accept. Do you agree?

Organise a class discussion on the topic, giving reasons for your point of view.

Pen it Down

Write a report in your local newspaper about the fast decreasing numbers of a particular species in your city that will deeply harm the environment in the long run. It could be a plant, an animal, a bird or a fish. Explain the problem and suggest measures to correct the situation.

21ST CENTURY Media Literacy

Self Assessment

Now I can

- understand how the destruction of forests may lead to the extinction of common animals.
- study idioms related to wolves and practise joining of sentences using participles.
- participate in a class discussion and write a newspaper report.

Read More

Moby Dick: This book by Herman Melville is about the whale hunter, Captain Ahab's quest to find the whale that had cost him his leg. The novel pits man against Nature as it follows Ahab's obsession to take revenge on the whale.

The Call of the Wild: This novel by Jack London is about the dog, Buck, who is stolen from its master and turned into a sledge dog. He has to remember the ways of the wild to survive in the harsh climate of Alaska and become the leader of its pack.

travelogue

15 A Short Walk in the Hindu Kush

Eric Newby

Let's Get Started

A. Travel often takes us to faraway lands. Have you heard about the places given below? Write the names in the continents where they are found.

1. Easter Island (South America)
2. The Alps (Europe)

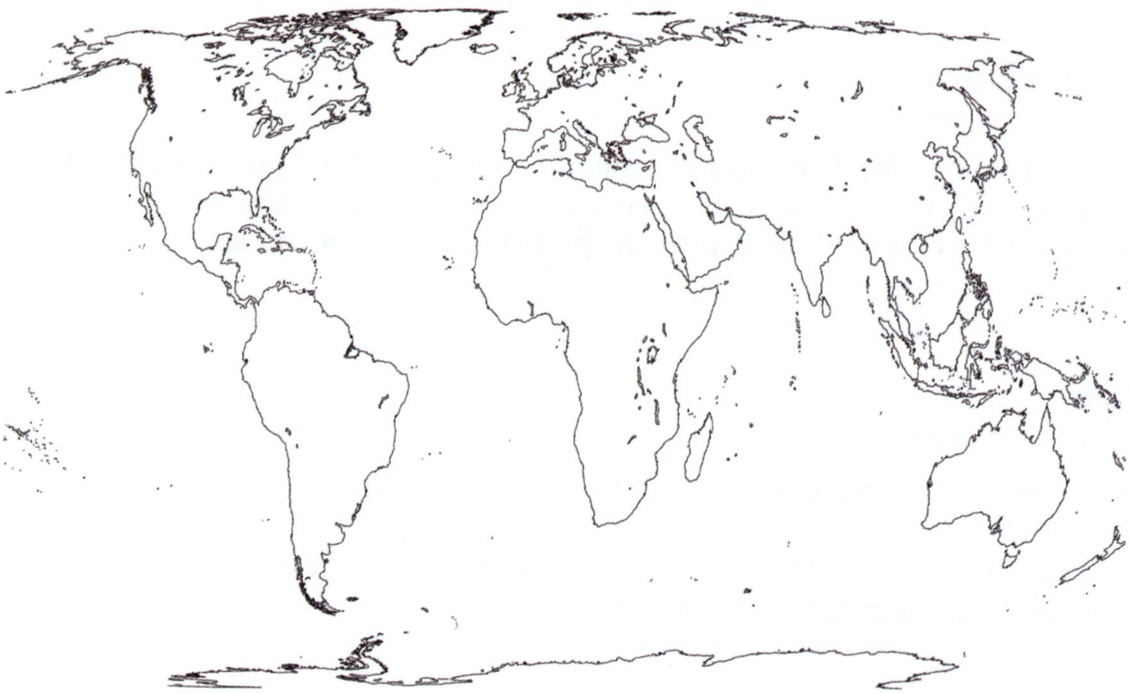

3. The Great Barrier Reef (Australia)
4. The Great Lakes (North America)
5. The Valley of the Kings (Africa)
6. Angkor Wat (Asia)

B. The best part about travel is that we meet unfamiliar people and learn about unusual customs. Can you name the countries where these tribes are present?

1. Aborigines
2. Inuits
3. Jarawas

HC **Learning and Awareness:** Evaluating our assumptions about life and situations around us

Reading

This passage is taken from* A Short Walk in the Hindu Kush, *a travelogue recounting Eric Newby's journey with his diplomat friend, Hugh Carless. They had set off in 1957 on an expedition to Nuristan, a remote area in Afghanistan that had almost never been visited by Europeans. Their aim was to climb Mir Samir, a difficult, unclimbed peak in the Hindu Kush mountain range. The book is a humorous account of their failed attempt to reach the peak. It describes their misadventures as they bumble through a difficult landscape, try to communicate with locals whose language and customs they often do not understand and frequently lose their temper with each other. In this extract, Newby and Carless reach Nuristan after a long and difficult journey and meet a group of shepherds.

The crest of the ridge, now immediately above our heads, was a wild confusion of loose blocks heaped one on top of the other. The way through the ridge was narrow, like the neck of a bottle. It was only by pushing and shoving that the horses were popped through to the other side like corks.

'**Kotal**-i-Chamar,' said the drivers.

It was the **col**; we were beyond the great divide; we were in Nuristan.

One more step and we would have fallen straight into it. We were huddled together, men and animals, on the edge of a cliff at the head of a **desolate** valley that stretched away downhill, a wilderness of bleak, brown **scree** with here and there a drift of dirty snow, until it was lost in haze.

The first part of the descent needed two men to each horse; one to lead, the other with a tight grip on the tail to brake hard at the bends; but once we were off the ridge, Hugh and I pressed on alone. For an hour and a half we followed the valley down and down. All the time it grew hotter; a little vegetation began to appear, pin-cushions of tough grass. Finally, we came out into a deep valley that ran north and south. It was green and open with a river running through it and on the meadow, grass cows, sheep and horses grazed **placidly**. Standing alone in the green meadow was a **solitary** ***aylaq***, a **bothy** and some stone cattle pens open to the sky. It seemed deserted; in the whole valley, there was no sign of anyone.

Kotal: mountain pass
col: the lowest point between two mountain peaks, a mountain pass
desolate: empty and without people living nearby
scree: small loose rocks
placidly: calmly and peacefully
solitary: only one
***aylaq*:** a local word for a shepherd camp
bothy: a small hut

What animals did the travellers see on the meadow?

After the miles of scree we had descended, the grass was like a carpet into which our feet sank. After the still airlessness of the upper valley, the breeze was as refreshing as a cool drink. Apart from the sighing of the wind and the sound of the river, a huge silence hung over the place. Men and horses were far behind. Feeling slightly nervous, we began to cross towards the *aylaq*.

We were a hundred yards from it when there was a shout and we saw our first Nuristanis. They came pouring out of the bothy and raced over the grass towards us at a tremendous pace, dozens of them. It seemed impossible that such a small building could have contained so many men. As they came bounding up, they gave an impression of being out of the past. They were all different, no two alike. They were tall and short, light-skinned and dark-skinned, brown-eyed and grey-eyed. There were men like gypsies with a lock of hair brought forward in ringlets on either side of the forehead. There were men with great bushy beards and moustaches that made them look like Arctic explorers. Some of the tallest (well over six feet) were broken-nosed, clean-shaven giants.

Did You Know? History

Alexander the Great is believed to have passed through Nuristan with a part of his army. Many Nuristanis claim to be descendants of Alexander.

All but those who were bare-headed wore the same flat Chitrali cap that Hugh had worn ever since we had left Kabul, only theirs were larger and more floppy, and the colour of porridge. They wore drab brown, collarless shirts and loose waistcoats. Their brown trousers reached to the middle of the calf and flapped loosely as their wearers pounded up the meadow. All were barefooted.

The next moment they were on us, uttering strange cries. Before we knew what was happening, we were being borne towards the *aylaq* with our feet barely touching the ground, each the centre of a mob, like distinguished visitors to a university.

What did the hosts set before the narrator and his friend?

We were made to sit on the floor and our hosts (for that was what they turned out to be) brought in two round wooden pots full of milk, which they set before us, together with a couple of large ladles. The pots held about half a gallon each, and seemed to be made from hollowed-out tree trunks. They were decorated with the same diamond pattern

I had noticed on the rugs. Both vessels and cutlery were of heroic **proportions**, fit for giants.

We were extremely thirsty. Hugh was already dipping into his pot.

'Do you think it's all right?' I asked him. 'They may have T.B.'

'Who?'

'The cows.'

'If we're going to get T.B., we've already got it,' he said. 'Besides, it's not cows' milk. I think it's goats' and sheep's mixed.'

The bothy was crammed to the point of suffocation with people all jabbering in an unknown tongue. I wondered if it were Bashguli. It was certainly unlike any other language I had ever heard. There was no way of discovering what it was.

proportions: size

quart: a unit for measuring liquids, equal to 1.14 litres

inquisitive: curious

After drinking nearly a **quart** of icy milk (the pots had just come out of the river), I felt as if I were going to burst. I put down my tree trunk. The boy sitting next to me picked up the ladle. 'Biloogh ow,' he grunted (that was what it sounded like) and began to forcibly feed me.

One of the older, full-bearded men, who seemed to have some sort of authority over the men, addressed Hugh in Persian.

Suddenly, he pointed to the north. 'Nikolai!' he said.

'Nikolai, Nikolai,' everyone said.

'Inghiliz, Inghiliz,' said Hugh.

'Nikolai, Nikolai.'

'Darn it. They think we're Russians,' he said. He was very upset.

Did You Know? G.K.

The Siah Posh are a major tribe of the Nuristan region, named after the black colour of their robes.

The halting conversation continued. It appeared that we were the first Europeans ever to come over the Pass. The Russians they had heard of; but the British were something new, outside their experience.

We were in the summer pastures of the Ramguli Katirs, a tribe of the black-robed Siah Posh. Here in the summer months, men of the tribe lived without their women, looking after the flocks and cattle, making curd and butter to store for the winter and for trade with the outside world.

All the time this recital was going on, we were being ransacked. I could feel **inquisitive** fingers on me, opening button flaps, groping in my pockets for my handkerchief, scrabbling at my watch strap.

We had already passed round several packets of cigarettes and a fight had developed for the empty packets. It was the silver paper they wanted. But what they really longed for were binoculars. They loved my camera, until they discovered that

Who were the Ramguli Katirs?

ingratiate: do things to make someone like you

frantically: hurriedly and in a worried manner

it was not a pair of binoculars, but they soon found Hugh's telescope and took it outside to try it.

In a world that has lost the capacity for wonderment, I found it very agreeable to meet people to whom it was possible to give pleasure so simply. Thinking to **ingratiate** myself still further with them, I handed over my watch. It was the pride of my heart (I, too, am easily pleased)—a brand-new Rolex that I had got in Geneva on the way out from England and was supposed to be proof against every kind of ill-treatment.

'Tell the headman,' I said to Hugh, 'that it will work under water.'

'He doesn't believe it.'

'All right. Tell him it will even work in that,' pointing to the cauldron which was giving off steam and gloggling noises.

Hugh told him. The headman said a few words to the young man who had the watch. Before I could stop him, he dropped it into the pot.

'He says he doesn't believe you,' said Hugh.

'Well, tell him to take it out! I don't believe it myself.' By now I was hanging over the thing, **frantically** fishing with the ladle.

'It's no good,' I said. 'They'll have to empty it.'

This time Hugh spoke somewhat more urgently to the headman.

'He says they don't want to. It's their dinner.'

At last somebody hooked it and brought it to the surface, covered with a sort of brown slime. Whatever it was for dinner had an extraordinary nasty appearance. The rescuer held it in the ladle. Though too hot to touch, it was still going. This made a great impression on everyone, myself included. Unfortunately, it made such an impression on the man himself that he refused to be parted from it and left the bothy.

'Where's he going?'

'He's going to try it in the river.'

At this moment, excited shouts and cries rose from outside. Our drivers had arrived. Everyone rushed out to greet them.

When the time came to leave, there was no sign of Hugh's telescope or my watch.

'I want my telescope,' Hugh told the headman.

'What about my watch?' I asked Hugh, when his telescope was finally produced from somewhere round the corner.

'He says the man who had it has gone away.'

'Well, tell him that he must bring him back.'

There was a further brief **parley**.

parley: discussion and negotiation

skulking: moving around secretly

scarcely: hardly

clenched: tightly closed

'He says the man wants to keep it.' Somehow, Hugh managed to make this sound like a reasonable request.

'WELL, HE CAN'T! GET IT BACK FOR ME! MAKE AN EFFORT!'

'It's *you* who should make the effort. It's really too much having to do your work all the time.'

I could have struck him at this moment. 'Damn it, you can hardly understand the man yourself and you speak fluent Persian. How do you expect me to make him understand anything?'

Just then I saw the man who had taken my watch **skulking** behind one of the walls of the *aylaq*. I went round the building the other way and came up behind him, and took hold of his wrists. Although he was without any apparent muscle, he was immensely strong.

'*Tok-tok*,' I said. At the same time, I looked down at my own wrist and nodded my head violently.

He began to laugh. I looked into his eyes; they were strange and mad. He had about him an air of **scarcely** controlled violence that I had noticed in some of the others inside the hut.

I saw that his right hand was **clenched** and I forced it open. Inside was my beautiful watch. He had washed it in the river. It was still going and it continued to do so.

As we left the *aylaq*, three more Nuristanis came running up the valley, moving over the ground in short steps but with unbelievable swiftness. All three had full brown beards; they wore short overcoats of a very dark brown. On their backs were slung empty pack frames.

'They have come up from the Ramgul to take the place of those who will go down with butter tomorrow morning,' said Abdul Ghiyas. [one of the duo's three local companions]

No one said goodbye to us. Some of the Nuristanis had already gone loping up the mountainside towards the flocks; the rest had gone back into the bothy. It was a characteristic of these people that their interest in strangers was exhausted almost as quickly as it was born.

Who was Abdul Ghiyas?

About the author

Eric Newby (1919–2006) was an English travel writer who wrote more than twenty books narrating his journeys in India, around the Mediterranean region and Ireland. He fought in World War II and was taken as a prisoner of war. He often used wry humour and understatement in his writing. Some of his best-known works include *The Last Grain Race* and *Love and War in the Apennines*.

Comprehension

Quick Recap

A. Answer the questions in a few lines.

1. How did the Nuristanis carry the writer and his friend to the bothy? Explain the figure of speech the writer uses to describe their actions.
2. What did the Nuristanis give the writer and his friend to drink? Why was the writer worried about it?
3. Why did the Nuristanis call them 'Nikolai'? What did this make the writer realise?
4. Which tribe did the Nuristanis belong to? What did they do in summer?
5. Why were the Nuristanis ransacking the travellers' bags? Explain the writer's comment about their actions.
6. As the writer left the bothy, who came running up the valley? Why had they come?
7. How did the writer get back his missing property?
8. Find two examples of similes in the travelogue.

B. Answer the questions with reference to context.

1. *The first part of the descent needed two men to each horse;*
   a. Where were the two travellers?
   b. What did the travellers have to pass through before beginning their descent?
   c. Describe the terrain that they had just crossed. What was the danger they faced?
   d. What did they see when they came down?
2. *They came pouring out of the bothy and raced over the grass towards us at a tremendous pace, dozens of them.*
   a. Who is being referred to as 'they'? Where did they come out from?
   b. Describe their physical features. What were they wearing?
   c. Why do you think the writer said that they seemed to be out of the past?
   d. What language did the writer think they were speaking?
3. *'Where's he going?'*
   'He's going to try it in the river.'
   a. Who are the speakers? Where were they?
   b. What is being referred to as 'it'? What was its special quality?
   c. Why had one of the speakers handed 'it' over? What unexpected thing had just been done to 'it'? Why?
   d. Why was 'he' going to 'try it' in the river?

Life Skills and Values — humour, importance of travel

Think and answer.

1. Discuss the humour in the incident with the writer's watch.
2. What kind of life did the people of Nuristan lead? What, according to you, was their most remarkable feature?
3. What do you think about the writer's attitude to the Nuristanis?

21ST CENTURY Critical Thinking

Way with Words

A. Find words from the travelogue to match the meanings.

1. gathered closely together, out of fear or cold
2. the act of coming down
3. air that is difficult to see through because it contains moisture
4. without any people
5. a large, deep pot for cooking over a fire
6. quickly, but in a disorganised manner
7. talking quickly and excitedly in a way that is difficult to understand

Compound Adjectives

B. Match the compound adjectives with the correct nouns and make sentences with five of the phrases.

Compound adjective	Nouns
1. record-breaking	a. friendship
2. long-standing	b. decision
3. last-minute	c. artefact
4. hand-made	d. sandals
5. open-toed	e. professor
6. quick-witted	f. performance
7. absent-minded	g. traveller
8. sun-tanned	h. remark

Grammar in Use

Joining Sentences: Infinitives and Gerunds

You know that infinitives take the form **to + verb**.
Example: We began **to cross** towards the *aylaq*.

You have also studied that gerunds take the **-ing** form of the verb. Like nouns, they can act as the subject or object in a sentence.

Example: **Travelling** makes me happy.

We can join sentences using infinitives and gerunds.
Examples: 1. I am going to the restaurant next door. I will have lunch there.
I am going to the restaurant next door **to have** lunch. (infinitive)

2. I jog every morning. It keeps me fit.
Jogging every morning keeps me fit. (gerund)

Join these sentences according to the given instructions.

1. He went to the library. He had to return the books. (begin: He went ...)
2. I went up to the principal. I wanted to ask her a question. (begin: I went ...)
3. Do not pluck flowers. It is forbidden. (begin: Plucking ...)
4. I play basketball. I prefer it over football. (begin: I prefer ...)
5. We should not give up. It is the most important thing. (begin: Not ...)
6. Sam sings in the shower. He enjoys it. (begin: Sam ...)
7. I will go to Europe next year. It is my plan. (begin: It is ...)
8. I want to act in a play. It is my dream. (begin: Acting ...)
9. Pam wants to know the test result. She has to wait till the end of the week. (begin: Pam ...)

Study Skills

Spell Check

We often add a double consonant where it is not needed and tend to drop one where it is required. Underline the words that are incorrect and write their correct spellings.

1. occurrence
2. tommorrow
3. parallel
4. embarass
5. recomend
6. accomodate
7. possession
8. referred
9. bookkeeper
10. dissappear
11. appologise
12. questionaire

Listening and Speaking

Listen to a conversation about a tourist asking for information from a travel agency. Now, imagine that you are going on a vacation to Africa, as a part of which, you want to go on a safari. Work in pairs to enact a conversation asking your travel agency for information and advice on the safari, and book the one that is suitable to you.

You can use the following points:

- location and cost
- hotel and travel bookings
- animals to be seen

Pen it Down

Look at the picture on the next page and write a paragraph on it. You can mention the following points:

- the performance and the audience
- the backdrop and region

- the costumes and masks worn by the performers
- the cultural nuances

HC Understanding similarities and oneness in humans

Self Assessment

Now I can

- read and understand the unexpected experiences of travellers in new lands.
- practise compound adjectives, and join sentences with infinitives and gerunds.
- enact a dialogue and write a paragraph on a picture.

Read More

Slowly Down the Ganges: This humorous travelogue by Eric Newby is about his journey with his wife along the 1200-mile length of the River Ganges from Haridwar to the Bay of Bengal. The couple deal with mishaps from the start as they travel on rickety boats, trains, buses and bullock carts, meeting colourful characters along the way.

Notes from a Small Island: This travel memoir by Bill Bryson is about his trip along the coast of England. Including detailed and funny descriptions of everyday life in towns and villages, it explores the oddities of the English character through conversations with shopkeepers, people at restaurants and other travellers.

16

War and Peace

Refugee Blues

W. H. Auden

Let's Get Started

SUSTAINABLE DEVELOPMENT GOALS

16 PEACE, JUSTICE AND STRONG INSTITUTIONS

The United Nations Sustainable Development Goal 16 seeks to promote peace, justice and strong institutions. However, in 2019, more than two-thirds of the total number of refugees in the world came from countries like Syria, Venezuela, Afghanistan and South Sudan.

Read this passage about refugees and fill in the blanks with the given words.

expelled	safeguards	asylum	law	violence	freedom
human rights	displaced	plight	governments	border	children

Refugees are people who have fled war, __________, conflict or persecution in their own countries and have crossed an international __________ to find safety in another country. They are defined and protected in international __________, and must not be __________ or returned to situations where their life and __________ are at risk. About 26.4 million people had fled their countries by 2020, and 82.4 million had been forcibly __________ from their homes, according to U.N. Refugee Agency (UNHCR). Almost 1 million __________ were born as refugees between 2018 and 2020. __________ across the world are working towards rehabilitation of refugees. The measures include __________ from being returned to danger, access to fair and efficient __________ procedures, and steps to ensure that their basic __________ __________ are respected while working out a long-term solution. Each year, the United Nations and people around the world recognize the __________ of refugees on June 20, World Refugee Day.

HC **Feelings:** Observing the desire for justice in society

Reading

A refugee is someone who flees their homeland because of war, religion, extreme poverty or social reasons. This poem refers to the Jewish Holocaust, which took place during World War II. Millions of Jewish people across Europe were killed by the Nazis, led by the German leader,

Adolf Hitler. The poem, composed in the form of a* blues *song, is about the ill-treatment and cruelty Jews had to face as they looked for a way to escape Europe.

Say this city has ten million souls,
Some are living in mansions, some are living in holes:
Yet there's no place for us, my dear, yet there's no place for us.

Once we had a country and we thought it fair,
Look in the atlas and you'll find it there:
We cannot go there now, my dear, we cannot go there now.

In the village churchyard there grows an old **yew**,
Every spring it blossoms anew:
Old passports can't do that, my dear, old passports can't do that.

The **consul** banged the table and said,
'If you've got no passport you're officially dead':
But we are still alive, my dear, but we are still alive.[1]

Went to a **committee**; they offered me a chair;
Asked me politely to return next year:
But where shall we go today, my dear, but where shall
we go today?

Came to a **public meeting**; the speaker got up and said;
'If we let them in, they will steal our daily bread':
He was talking of you and me, my dear, he was talking
of you and me.

Thought I heard the thunder rumbling in the sky;
It was Hitler over Europe, saying, 'They must die':
O we were in his mind, my dear, O we were in his mind.

Saw a **poodle** in a jacket fastened with a pin,
Saw a door opened and a cat let in:
But they weren't German Jews, my dear, but they
weren't German Jews.

Went down the harbour and stood upon the **quay**,
Saw the fish swimming as if they were free:
Only ten feet away, my dear, only ten feet away.

Literary term

1. This is an example of **irony**. Though the speaker is alive, he is told by someone else that he is 'officially dead'.

Did You Know? History

Although Jews have lived in Europe for over 2000 years, they have often faced hostility. Before World War II, many found refuge in friendly countries. As the war approached, this became difficult. During the war, death squads searched for and killed Jews.

blues: a slow, sad song, historically associated with African Americans working on slave plantations

yew: an evergreen tree

consul: a government official who is the representative of a country in a foreign city

committee: (here) an organisation to help refugees

public meeting: (here) meetings held in countries receiving Jewish people to discuss the help that could be offered

poodle: a small species of dog with thick, curly hair, typically associated with rich people

quay: a platform in a harbour on which one can stand and watch boats come in

What didn't the birds have?

Walked through a wood, saw the birds in the trees;
They had no politicians and sang at their ease:
They weren't the human race, my dear, they weren't the
human race.

Dreamed I saw a building with a thousand floors,
A thousand windows and a thousand doors:
Not one of them was ours, my dear, not one of them was ours.

Stood on a great plain in the falling snow;
Ten thousand soldiers marched to and fro:
Looking for you and me, my dear, looking for you and me.

About the poet

Wystan Hugh Auden (1907–1973) was an English poet and one of the most influential poets of the twentieth century. His poems have a strong political and social message. He believed that the human spirit survives best in an atmosphere of tolerance and compassion. Some of his best-known poems are 'Spain' and 'Museé des Beaux Arts'.

Comprehension

Quick Recap

A. Answer the questions in a few lines.

1. How many people are believed to be living in the city?
2. How does the poet contrast an old yew tree with the passports of Jews?
3. What did the consul tell the speaker and his companion about their status?
4. Explain the line, 'Some are living in mansions, some are living in holes:'
5. How was the speaker treated by people in other countries where he went seeking refuge?
6. Which lines in the poem indicate that there were no homes for Jews, even though there was enough housing?
7. What were the various locations that the speaker went to?
8. What were the soldiers doing on the great plain? Why?

B. Answer the questions with reference to context.

1. *Once we had a country and we thought it fair,/Look in the atlas and you'll find it there:/ We cannot go there now, my dear, we cannot go there now.*
   a. Who is the speaker in these lines? Whom does he address as 'dear'?
   b. Which country is the speaker referring to? Why can't he go there anymore?

c. Explain the contradiction in the second and third lines.

d. Explain the use of repetition in the last line of the quoted stanza.

2. *Thought I heard the thunder rumbling in the sky;/It was Hitler over Europe, saying, 'They must die':/ O we were in his mind, my dear, O we were in his mind.*

   a. What does 'thunder' represent here? Explain in your own words.

   b. Whom was Hitler referring to as 'They'?

   c. Explain the phrase 'we were in his mind'.

3. *Walked through a wood, saw the birds in the trees;/They had no politicians and sang at their ease:/ They weren't the human race, my dear, they weren't the human race.*

   a. What kind of lives do the birds lead?

   b. How are the birds better than the human race?

   c. Which are the other non-human creatures mentioned in the poem? How is their condition better than that of the Jews?

Life Skills and Values racial discrimination, misery of displacement, surviving war

Think and answer.

1. What does the title of the poem mean? Explain its significance.
2. Which are the striking images in the poem? Explain them in your own words.
3. How does the poem convey the misery of displaced people? Do you think it is relevant in today's world? How?

21ST CENTURY Critical Thinking

Way with Words

Words Related to The Holocaust

A. Complete the passage with the given words/phrases.

World War II	Holocaust	Nazis	occupation	human dignity	victims	inflicted

Anne Frank's *Diary of a Young Girl* is a book about the Jewish ______________ from a young girl's point of view. Anne and her family were forced to hide to avoid capture during the German ______________ of Holland. They spent two years in the 'secret annex' of a warehouse. Her diary offers a glimpse into the horrors ______________ on Jewish people by the ______________. Anne Frank is one of the most discussed Jewish ______________ of ______________. President John F. Kennedy of America discussed Anne in a 1961 speech. He said that of all the people who have spoken for ______________ in times of great suffering and loss, no voice is stronger than that of Anne Frank.

Using Suffixes to Form Nationalities

We usually form adjectives relating to countries, languages and races by adding the following suffixes:

-ish: British, Spanish | **-i**: Bangladeshi, Iraqi | **-an**: German, Tibetan

-ic: Icelandic, Arabic | **-ese**: Portuguese, Japanese | **-n**: Bolivian, Indian

There are also exceptions, such as 'Peruvian' (from Peru) and 'Swiss' (from Switzerland).

B. Write the adjectives used to describe the nationalities of people from these countries.

1. Chile
2. Vietnam
3. Brazil
4. Ireland
5. Israel
6. Finland
7. The Netherlands
8. New Zealand
9. Saudi Arabia
10. China
11. Mongolia
12. Russia
13. Nepal
14. Canada
15. France
16. Egypt

Grammar in Use

Determiners: Quantifiers and Distributives

You have studied about determiners earlier. Quantifiers and distributives are two of the several types of determiners.

Quantifiers include **many**, **more**, **much**, **least** and **less**. They are used to describe uncountable nouns.

Examples: The building housed **many** people.
The refugees had suffered **much** hardship.

Distributives include **each**, **every**, **either** and **neither**. They describe countable nouns and are always used with a singular noun. **Either** and **neither** refer to one part of a pair.

Examples: **Every** spring it blossoms anew.
Neither committee provided a solution to the refugee's problem.

A. Complete the sentences with the following determiners.

least little much each all either neither

1. ________ students should report for the Knowledge Camp by 9 a.m. on Monday.
2. We can offer ________ help to the trapped miners tonight. We have to wait for daybreak.
3. Please contribute to the cause, even if it's the ________ amount possible.
4. ________ suspect is innocent of this crime, so the judge is letting them walk free.
5. ________ of the two sweaters is mine.
6. ________ person who had gathered for the protest was given a candle.
7. ________ water has flowed under the bridge since our last meeting.

PUNCTUATION: PARENTHESES, ELLIPSIS AND HYPHEN

When we want to give additional information that cannot be included within a sentence, we put it within brackets. These brackets are called **parentheses**.

Example: Maya and Manish **(who are actually twins)** do not like talking about each other.

An **ellipsis** consists of three consecutive periods. It is written as '...'. It indicates the omission of unnecessary words. It is also used to indicate an incomplete thought, in informal language.

Example: If only I had gone home earlier **...** Oh well, it does not matter.

Phrases that serve as compound adjectives should always be **hyphenated**.

Example: Her **mother-in-law** is the headmistress of a reputed school. (not *mother in law*)

B. Rewrite the sentences using correct punctuation.

1. The culprits who escaped to the UK are being searched for by the police.
2. I wish we had bought the black sofa instead of the blue one. Well, the blue one isn't bad either.
3. Our France returned neighbours are quite well to do.
4. The ten feet tall mango tree in our backyard my grandfather planted it as a young man was cut down today.
5. The king of the forest long may he live wishes to meet you.

Study Skills

Pronounce Well

A **diphthong** is a sound consisting of two distinct vowel sounds.

In a diphthong, one vowel sound gradually changes into another within the same syllable.

Examples: toil, cry, break

These are the five common diphthongs in English:

[ei] gr**ey** [ai] n**i**ce [au] all**ow** [oi] ann**oy** [ou] her**o**

Write the following words under the diphthong with the same pronunciation. Then, write one more word of your own in each column.

stay	climate	crowd	exploit	control	bounce	blind
destroy	poison	oyster	analyse	race	neighbour	cycle
focus	brow	although	toast	foul	betray	

[ei]	[ai]	[au]	[oi]	[ou]

Listening and Speaking

Listen to a passage about a brave man who saved Jewish people at the height of WW II. Then, write whether these sentences are true (T) or false (F). Correct the false statements.

1. The brave man who helped several Jews was a German called Oskar. ☐
2. He saved 1000 Jews by employing them in his garment factories. ☐
3. Initially, he was interested only in profits, but changed his mind later. ☐
4. He had to bribe Nazi officials by offering them a share in his factories. ☐
5. After the war, the man went to West Germany, where he became bankrupt. ☐
6. His story was made into a film by Stephen King. ☐

Pen it Down

People being forced to leave their homes for various reasons is a harsh reality in today's world. Form groups of four, with each group taking up a contemporary topic related to the theme of displacement. Research the topic and write a poem about it, focusing on the hardships and suffering of common people.

21ST CENTURY Information Literacy

These are some of the issues you could focus on:

- people fleeing war in their own country
- natural disasters destroying people's homes

Read out your poems in class.

21ST CENTURY Creativity

Self Assessment

Now I can

- understand the suffering of Jews during the Holocaust.
- practise determiners, and use parentheses, ellipsis and hyphen.
- pronounce diphthongs, and research and write a poem on a given topic.

Read More

Maus: This graphic novel by American cartoonist Art Spiegelman describes the experiences of the author's father as a survivor of the Nazi concentration camps. It metaphorically depicts the Jews as mice and the Nazis as cats.

Once: This book by Morris Gleitzman is about ten-year-old Felix, who is hiding from the Nazis in a Catholic orphanage. Not knowing the dangers of the outside world, he sets out on a journey to find his parents and warn them of danger, and lands up in the heart of Nazi-occupied Poland.

Short Story

17

Humour

My Financial Career

Stephen Leacock

Let's Get Started

One of the easiest and most effective ways to create humour is to depict everyday activities in a funny way. Do you remember your first day at school, or the day you forgot to bring your homework to class? These ordinary experiences can be made humorous by using exaggeration, witty phrases and hilarious descriptions.

Read the paragraph below. Underline and write the instances of humour in the correct columns.

It was almost time to submit the exam scripts and I had not written a word! All that I had managed to do was write my name and the subject at the top, along with a desperate attempt to call upon divine help manifested in three religious symbols. I was not particularly a believer of God but since no help was forthcoming from my grey cells, I realised I needed someone more powerful to set things right. But none of those symbols transformed themselves into miracles and I was lost. Looking around I saw Toby writing on his tenth sheet furiously, the anger of sleepless nights on his face. Maria was writing slowly as if she was running out of words, her tongue curled up at the edge of her lips. Willie was busy drawing something—what could one draw for a test on grammar and vocabulary? I had no idea.

I looked back at my page of pristine white and began to feel sorry for my teacher who would be greeted with this empty script. She took our failures as personal failures and my paper would reduce her to tears! Just then, the bell rang and the invigilator came to collect my script. He saw my empty paper and said, 'You didn't attempt any of the questions? What were you doing for the last one hour?' Hesitatingly, I said, 'I was busy wondering the sort of exams witches and vampires sit for…' The invigilator shouted, 'What nonsense! Well, how long did you wonder?' 'Well, I almost got my answer—witches sit for spelling tests and vampires sit for blood tests.'

The invigilator glared at me and then stormed off.

Exaggeration	Wit	Hilarious Descriptions	Pun

Learning and Awareness: Evaluating our assumptions and preconditions about life and situations around us

Reading

Have you ever been to a bank, with your elders? Did you find the hustle and bustle scary? Do you know how to open a bank account? Read this hilarious story to find out.

When I go into a bank, I get **rattled**. The clerks rattle me; the **wickets** rattle me; the sight of the money rattles me; everything rattles me.

What idea did the narrator have about opening an account?

rattled: nervous

wicket: (here) a small window generally fitted with a grating or glass pane, used as a means of communication in a bank

threshold: entrance

transact: carry out, conduct

shambled in: moved in an awkward manner

sepulchral: serious or sad, somewhat frightening

The moment I cross the **threshold** of a bank and attempt to **transact** business there, I become an irresponsible idiot.

I knew this beforehand, but my salary had been raised to fifty dollars a month and I felt that the bank was the only place for it.

So I **shambled in** and looked timidly round at the clerks. I had an idea that a person about to open an account must consult the manager.

I went up to a wicket marked 'Accountant.' The accountant was a tall, cool devil. The very sight of him rattled me. My voice was **sepulchral**.

'Can I see the manager?' I said, and added solemnly, 'alone.' I don't know why I said 'alone.'

'Certainly,' said the accountant, and fetched him.

The manager was a grave, calm man. I held my fifty-six dollars clutched in a crumpled ball in my pocket.

'Are you the manager?' I said. God knows I didn't doubt it.

'Yes,' he said.

'Can I see you,' I asked, 'alone?' I didn't want to say 'alone' again, but without it the thing seemed self-evident.

The manager looked at me in some alarm. He felt that I had an awful secret to reveal.

'Come in here,' he said, and led the way to a private room. He turned the key in the lock.

'We are safe from interruption here,' he said, 'sit down.'

We both sat down and looked at each other. I found no voice to speak.

'You are one of Pinkerton's men, I presume,' he said.

He had gathered from my mysterious manner that I was a detective. I knew what he was thinking, and it made me worse.

'No, not from Pinkerton's,' I said, seeming to **imply** that I came from a **rival** agency. 'To tell the truth,' I went on, as if I had been prompted to lie about it, 'I am not a detective at all. I have come to open an account. I intend to keep all my money in this bank.'

Did You Know? **G.K.**

Pinkertons Detectives was a very popular private detective agency established in the United States in 1850. This agency also supplied security persons and was known for the speed and efficiency of their services.

The manager looked relieved but still serious; he concluded now that I was a son of Baron Rothschild or a young Gould.

Why did the manager think the narrator to be a detective?

'A large account, I suppose,' he said.

'Fairly large,' I whispered. 'I propose to deposit fifty-six dollars now and fifty dollars a month regularly.'

The manager got up and opened the door. He called to the accountant.

'Mr Montgomery,' he said unkindly loud, 'this gentleman is opening an account, he will deposit fifty-six dollars. Good morning.'

I rose.

A big iron door stood open at the side of the room.

'Good morning,' I said, and stepped into the safe.

'Come out,' said the manager coldly, and showed me the other way.

I went up to the accountant's wicket and poked the ball of money at him with a quick **convulsive** movement as if I were doing a **conjuring** trick.

My face was **ghastly** pale.

'Here,' I said, 'deposit it.' The tone of the words seemed to mean, 'Let us do this painful thing while the fit is on us.'

He took the money and gave it to another clerk.

He made me write the sum on a slip and sign my name in a book. I no longer knew what I was doing. The bank swam before my eyes.

'Is it deposited?' I asked in a hollow, **vibrating** voice.

imply: indicate indirectly

rival: enemy

convulsive: quick and confused

conjuring: magic

ghastly: terrible

vibrating: shaking

impression: a vague idea or belief

'It is,' said the accountant.

'Then I want to draw a cheque.'

My idea was to draw out six dollars of it for present use. Someone gave me a chequebook through a wicket and someone else began telling me how to write it out. The people in the bank had the **impression** that I was an invalid millionaire. I wrote something on the cheque and thrust it in at the clerk. He looked at it.

'What! are you drawing it all out again?' he asked in surprise. Then I realised that I had written fifty-six instead of six. I was too far gone to reason now. I had a feeling that it was impossible to explain the thing. All the clerks had stopped writing to look at me.

Reckless with misery, I made a plunge.

What mistake did the narrator make while writing the cheque?

'Yes, the whole thing.'

'You want to withdraw your money from the bank?'

'Every cent of it.'

'Are you not going to deposit any more?' said the clerk, astonished.

'Never.'

An idiot hope struck me that they might think something had insulted me while I was writing the cheque and that I had changed my mind. I made a wretched attempt to look like a man with a fearfully quick temper.

The clerk prepared to pay the money.

'How will you have it?' he said.

'What?'

'How will you have it?'

'Oh'—I caught his meaning and answered without even trying to think—'in fifties.'

He gave me a fifty-dollar bill.

'And the six?' he asked dryly.

'In sixes,' I said.

He gave it me and I rushed out.

As the big door swung behind me, I caught the echo of a roar of laughter that went up to the ceiling of the bank. Since then I bank no more. I keep my money in cash in my trousers pocket and my savings in silver dollars in a sock.

About the author

Stephen Leacock (1869–1944) was a famous Canadian writer and lecturer, whose books include the fascinating *Literary Lapses* and *Nonsense Novel*. His stories are based on ordinary but amusing situations that anyone may face. He believed that humour was the ultimate expression of a kind-hearted man.

Comprehension

Quick Recap

A. Read the sentences and state whether they are true (T) or false (F). Correct the false sentences.

1. The narrator got a new salary of 60 dollars a month. ☐
2. He wanted to deposit the money at the bank. ☐
3. The narrator was very confident about going to the bank. ☐
4. The name of the accountant was Montgomery. ☐
5. The narrator withdrew 60 dollars. ☐

B. Answer the questions with reference to context.

1. *The moment I cross the threshold of a bank and attempt to transact business there, I become an irresponsible idiot.*
   a. What is the narrator's state of mind when he enters the bank?
   b. What 'rattles' him?
   c. Where does the humour originate from in this sentence?
2. *'You are one of Pinkerton's men, I presume,' he said. He had gathered from my mysterious manner that I was a detective.*
   a. Who is being referred to as 'he' here?
   b. What is the 'mysterious manner' of the narrator, being referred to here?
   c. What misunderstanding had the mysterious manner caused?
   d. How is the misunderstanding humorous? When was it sorted?
3. *Reckless with misery, I made a plunge.*
   'Yes, the whole thing.'
   a. What caused the narrator to be 'reckless with misery'?
   b. What is meant by the word 'plunge'? What plunge did he make?
   c. Who was checking with the narrator? What was the reaction of the others at the bank?

C. Complete this character sketch, choosing sentences from the story that matches with the narrator's personality traits. One has been done for you.

Narrator

- foolish
- **nervous**: *The clerks rattle me; the wickets rattle me; the sight of the money rattles me; everything rattles me.*
- not wealthy
- not confident

Life Skills and Values — empathising with others, handling stress

Think and answer.

1. Do you identify with the plight of the narrator at the bank and feel sorry for him? Why?
2. In what way is the title of the story a comment on the events in the story? Give examples to bring out the irony of the title.
3. Have you ever found yourself in a similar situation, when you acted foolishly because of stress? How did you deal with it?

Way with Words

Idioms Related to Anxiety

A. Complete the sentences with these idioms related to anxiety.

scared the daylights out of	sent a chill down everyone's spine	bundle of nerves
shaking like a leaf	scared out of our wits	like a cat on a hot tin roof

1. By the time my name was called out for the talent show, I was ______________.
2. The sight of the veiled woman ______________ the residents of the hostel.
3. The girl was ______________ before she went up to the podium to give her speech.
4. The eerie howling of the wind at night ______________.
5. Mahima was ______________ the entire week before her exam results were declared.
6. We were ______________ when his parachute refused to open during air-diving.

B. Complete the sentences with the correct words. Use a dictionary to find the meaning of the difficult words. One is done for you.

1. The soulful ___*elegy*___ (~~elegy~~/obituary) composed by the poet was selected for the collection of poems.
2. The scientist was upset by the ________________ (disapproving/humiliating) comments made by his closest colleagues.
3. You must ________________ (ensure/insure) your new car as soon as possible.
4. She looked at her mother ________________ (furtively/insolently) as she entered her home two hours after the expected time.
5. The ________________ (accusing/amusing) remarks made by her sisters brought tears to Cinderella's eyes.
6. The fort we visited today is ________________ (older/elder) than the palace we visited yesterday.

Grammar in Use

Transformation of Sentences

You have learnt several ways of rewriting sentences without changing their meanings. Now, look at the following three types of sentence structures. The structures in each type can be used interchangeably.

1. **as soon as .../no sooner ... than .../hardly had ... when ...**

   Examples: **As soon as** he wrote the cheque, he realised he had put down the entire amount.
   No sooner did he write the cheque **than** he realised that he had put down the entire amount.
   Hardly had he written the cheque **when** he realised that he had put down the entire amount.

2. **although .../in spite of .../despite ...**

   Examples: **Although** he had deposited only fifty-six dollars, he withdrew the entire sum.
   In spite of depositing only fifty-six dollars, he withdrew the entire sum.
   Despite depositing only fifty-six dollars, he withdrew the entire sum.

3. **not only ... but also .../not only ... as well/not only ... too/besides ... also ...**

   Examples: **Not only** did he withdraw the entire sum **but also** announced that he would never deposit money again.
   Not only did he withdraw the entire sum, he also announced that he would never deposit money again **as well**.
   Not only did he withdraw the entire sum, he also announced that he would never deposit money again **too**.
   Besides withdrawing the entire sum, he **also** announced that he would never deposit money again.

Rewrite the sentences according to the instruction given, without changing the meaning.

1. As soon as the examinations began, the power cuts started. (begin: No sooner ...)
2. Besides being the director's debut film, it was also based on his own novel. (use 'Not only ... too')
3. Despite being warned, they went for a swim on the cloudy day. (begin: In spite of ...)
4. Hardly had we checked in our baggage when the airline announced that the flight was cancelled. (begin: As soon as ...)
5. Although it was a holiday, we had to go to school for extra classes. (begin: Despite ...)
6. No sooner had the baby seen its mother than it started smiling. (begin: Hardly had ...)
7. In spite of being hungry, the poor man gave his food to the hungry child. (begin: Although ...)
8. Besides playing cricket, basketball and volleyball, he also swims. (use 'Not only ... but also')

Study Skills

Use Your Dictionary

An **eponym** is a word taken from the name of a real, fictional or mythical character.

In an eponym, the name of the person or character related to a discovery, phenomenon or thing is used to refer to it.

Example: The term 'Achilles heel' an eponym. It is often used to describe a weak point or fault in somebody's character, which can be attacked by other people. It comes from the mighty Greek hero, Achilles who was dipped in the river Styx by his mother, making him invincible, except for the part of his heel where his mother held him. He was eventually killed after being wounded in his heel.

A. Use your dictionary to match the meanings with the eponyms.

A	B
1. a seemingly impossible or difficult task	a. maverick
2. a harsh legal code	b. limerick
3. a ballpoint pen	c. Biro
4. an independent person who refuses to follow social rules	d. cardigan
5. a knitted garment	e. herculean
6. a short, humorous poem	f. draconian

B. Now, find the names from which these eponyms were derived.

Listening and Speaking

A. Listen to the passage carefully. Choose the correct options to complete the sentences.

1. Mr Appin had reached his goal of teaching Tobermory ________________.
   a. human sounds b. scientific experiments
   c. human speech d. how to drink tea

2. Mr Appin was successful because Tobermory ________________.

a. was not a backward adult
b. was a 'Beyond Cat' of extraordinary intelligence
c. had excellent memory
d. was his favourite cat

3. Lady Blemley wanted the cat in the room because ________________.

a. she did not believe in miracles
b. she thought Mr Appin was joking
c. she wanted to judge the cat
d. she wanted proof that Mr Appin was successful

4. By the end of Mr Appin's experiment, Tobermory could ________________.

a. speak in a horrible natural voice
b. speak in easy sentences of one syllable
c. only yawn
d. not speak at all

5. The phrase 'jumped out of my skin' means ________________.

a. to be excited
b. to be scared
c. to be in an accident
d. to be in an argument

6. Tobermory's response to Sir Wilfrid showed that he ________________.

a. was extraordinarily lazy
b. disliked company and did what he pleased
c. was an obedient pet
d. was a scary animal

Pen it Down

Read these instructions. Think of where you would find them.

- Wet the hair and apply a small amount of shampoo. Work into a lather. Rinse and repeat.
- Mix two teaspoons of cocoa powder with two spoons of sugar. Add a little cold milk and make a smooth paste. Now add a cup of hot milk and stir vigorously till you get a smooth blend.

While giving instructions or describing a process, we must remember to be precise and concise. We should brainstorm the steps or stages in a process and then use the language that can convey the information without causing any confusion.

Write the process of opening a bank account and depositing a cheque. Make sure you use some of the transition words given in the box to link the different steps of the process.

at first	after that	make sure that
next	finally	before
meanwhile	avoid doing	be careful not to

You may include these details when you write about the process:

- choosing the bank
- giving personal information
- consenting to the bank's policies
- funding your account

Self Assessment

Now I can

- read and understand a humorous story about experiences at a bank.
- use idioms related to anxiety, differentiate between difficult words, and transform sentences without changing their meaning.
- match eponyms with their meanings, and write a process.

Read More

Three men in a Boat: This story by Jerome K Jerome talks about an epic journey down the river Thames that three young and impressionable men decide to undertake. They are accompanied by a dog, and their journey is a series of comic misadventures.

The Secret Diary of Adrian Mole: In this story by Sue Townsend, Adrian Mole is a sensitive and emotional teenager who lives with his eccentric parents in Leicester. His longings for an intellectual life and the funny situations they land him into are painstakingly captured in a secret diary.

18

The Tragedy of Julius Caesar

William Shakespeare

Let's Get Started

A. Match the names of these ancient conquerors with the civilisations they came from.

Name	Civilisation
1. Alexander •	• a. Kushan
2. Augustus Caesar •	• b. Greek
3. Cyrus •	• c. Turk-Mongol
4. Kanishka •	• d. Persian
5. Timur •	• e. Roman

B. Historical fiction comprises a make-believe story based in historical facts. The story may focus around a famous historical event or person. The writer creates his/her own version of the finer details of history, all the while adhering to the fundamental facts of history.

Have you read any such instances of historical fiction? What did you find interesting in them?

Work in pairs and think of at least three important traits of historical fiction that make it interesting. Write them in the space given.

____

____

____

HC **Feelings:** Participating in society – helping in maintaining systems

Reading

This scene is taken from Shakespeare's play about the assassination of the Roman dictator, Julius Caesar. Afraid of Caesar's growing influence, a group of Senators, including Caesar's most trusted friend, Brutus and Cassius think that he may become king. They hatch a plot to overthrow him, and Caesar is assassinated in the Roman Senate. Afterwards, his supporter Mark

Antony cleverly turns the citizens of Rome against the conspirators. This scene, known for the speeches of Antony and Brutus, shows how powerful words can be in swaying public opinion.

Characters

Brutus, member of Roman Senate and Julius Caesar's closest friend

Marc Antony, Roman general and supporter of Julius Caesar

Citizens of Rome

satisfied: be content with a satisfactory explanation

give me audience: listen to me

part the numbers: separate the crowd

rendered: given

severally: separately

pulpit: raised platform

lovers: (here) good friends

censure: judge

senses: understanding

Who hatched a plot against Caesar?

Act 3, Scene 2: The forum

Enter Brutus and Cassius, and a throng of citizens

Citizens We will be **satisfied**; let us be satisfied.

Brutus Then follow me, and **give me audience**, friends.
Cassius, go you into the other street,
And **part the numbers**.
Those that will hear me speak, let 'em stay here;
Those that will follow Cassius, go with him;
And public reasons shall be **rendered**
Of Caesar's death.

First citizen I will hear Brutus speak.

Second citizen I will hear Cassius; and compare their reasons,
When **severally** we hear them rendered.

Exit Cassius with some of the citizens. Brutus goes into the ***pulpit***

Third citizen The noble Brutus is ascended: silence!

Brutus Be patient till the last. Romans, countrymen and **lovers**! Hear me for my cause, and be silent, that you may hear: believe me for mine honour, and have respect to mine honour, that you may believe: **censure** me in your wisdom, and awake your **senses**, that you may the better judge. If there be any in this assembly, any dear friend of Caesar's, to him I say, that Brutus' love to Caesar was no less than his. If then that friend demand why Brutus rose against Caesar, this is my answer: –Not that I loved Caesar less, but that I loved Rome more. Had you rather Caesar were living and die all slaves, than that Caesar were dead, to live all free men? As

Caesar loved me, I weep for him; as he was **fortunate**, I rejoice at it; as he was valiant, I honour him: but, as he was ambitious, I slew him.[1] There is tears for his love; joy for his fortune; honour for his valour and death for his ambition. Who is here so base that would be a **bondman**? If any, speak; for him have I offended. Who is here so **rude** that would not be a Roman? If any, speak; for him have I offended. Who is here so vile that will not love his country? If any, speak; for him have I offended.
I pause for a reply.

All None, Brutus, none.

Brutus Then none have I offended. I have done no more to Caesar than you shall do to Brutus. The question of his death is **enrolled** in the **Capitol**; his **glory** not **extenuated**, wherein he was worthy, nor his offences **enforced**, for which he suffered death.

Enter Antony and others, with Caesar's body

Here comes his body, mourned by Mark Antony: who, though he had no hand in his death, shall receive the benefit of his dying, a place in the **commonwealth**; as which of you shall not? With this I depart,—that, as I slew my best lover for the good of Rome, I have the same dagger for myself, when it shall please my country to need my death.

All Live, Brutus! live, live!

First citizen Bring him with triumph home unto his house.

Second citizen Give him a statue with his ancestors.

Third citizen Let him be Caesar.

Brutus My countrymen,—

Second citizen Peace, silence! Brutus speaks.

First citizen Peace, ho!

Brutus Good countrymen, let me depart alone,
And, for my sake, stay here with Antony:
Do **grace** to Caesar's corpse, and grace his speech
Tending to Caesar's glories; which Mark Antony,
By our permission, is allow'd to make.
I do entreat you, not a man depart,
Save I alone, till Antony have spoke.

Exit

Literary term

1.This is the **climax** of the speech. Through a series of words, 'weep', 'rejoice', 'honour' and 'slew', there is an increasing dramatic effect, till the last word, which is the peak of the dramatic moment.

What, according to Brutus, was documented in the Capitol?

fortunate: successful
bondman: slave
rude: uncivilised
enrolled: recorded
Capitol: the Senate House. It was the seat of power in Rome. In the play, Caesar is assassinated here.
glory: noble deeds
extenuated: lessened
enforced: made larger
commonwealth: republic
grace: honour
tending: referring

First citizen Stay, ho! and let us hear Mark Antony.

Third citizen Let him go up into the public chair;
We'll hear him. Noble Antony, go up.

Antony For Brutus' sake, I am **beholding** to you.

Goes into the pulpit

Fourth citizen What does he say of Brutus?

Third citizen He says, for Brutus' sake, he finds himself beholding to us all.

Fourth citizen 'Twere best he speak no harm of Brutus here.

First citizen This Caesar was a tyrant.

Third citizen Nay, that's certain: We are **blest** that Rome is rid of him.

Second citizen Peace! Let us hear what Antony can say.

Antony You gentle Romans,—

Citizens Peace, ho! Let us hear him.

Antony Friends, Romans, countrymen, **lend me your ears**;
I come to bury Caesar, not to praise him.
The evil that men do lives after them;
The good is oft **interred** with their bones;
So let it be with Caesar. The noble Brutus
Hath told you Caesar was ambitious:
If it were so, it was a **grievous** fault,
And grievously hath Caesar answered it.
Here, **under leave** of Brutus and the rest—
For Brutus is an honourable man[2]
So are they all, all honourable men—
Come I to speak in Caesar's funeral.
He was my friend, faithful and just to me:
But Brutus says he was ambitious;
And Brutus is an honourable man.
He hath brought many captives home to Rome
Whose ransoms did the **general coffers** fill:
Did this in Caesar seem ambitious?
When that the poor have cried, Caesar hath wept:
Ambition should be made of **sterner** stuff:
Yet Brutus says he was ambitious;

Who came to bury Caesar?

beholding: indebted

blest: blessed

lend me your ears: listen to me

interred: buried

grievous: unforgivable

under leave: with permission

general coffers: public treasury

sterner: stronger

Literary term

2. This is an example of **irony**. Antony calls the conspirators 'honourable' even though he means the opposite.

And Brutus is an honourable man.
You all did see that on the Lupercal
I thrice presented him a kingly crown,
Which he did thrice refuse: was this ambition?
Yet Brutus says he was ambitious;
And, sure, he is an honourable man.
I speak not to **disprove** what Brutus spoke,
But here I am to speak what I do know.
You all did love him once, not without cause:
What cause **withholds** you then, to mourn for him?
O judgment![3] Thou art fled to brutish beasts,
And men have lost their reason. Bear with me;
My heart is in the coffin there with Caesar,
And I must pause till it come back to me.

First citizen **Methinks** there is much reason in his sayings.

Second citizen If thou consider rightly of the matter, Caesar has had great wrong.

Second citizen Poor soul! His eyes are red as fire with weeping.

Third citizen There's not a nobler man in Rome than Antony.

Fourth citizen Now **mark** him, he begins again to speak.

Antony **But** yesterday the word of Caesar might
Have **stood against** the world; now lies he there.
And none so poor to do him reverence.
O masters, if I **were disposed** to stir
Your hearts and minds to mutiny and rage,
I should do Brutus wrong, and Cassius wrong,
Who, you all know, are honourable men:
I will not do them wrong; I rather choose
To wrong the dead, to wrong myself and you,
Than I will wrong such honourable men.
But here's a **parchment** with the seal of Caesar;
I found it in his closet, 'tis his will:
Let but the commons hear this **testament**—
Which, pardon me, I do not mean to read—
And they would go and kiss dead Caesar's wounds
And dip their **napkins** in his sacred blood,

Did You Know? History

The feast of Lupercal was an ancient Roman festival that celebrated fertility.

What had Antony presented Caesar with?

Literary term

3. This is an **apostrophe**. Here, Antony breaks away from his audience and speaks directly to 'Judgement', or man's ability to use his reason, which seems to be lost.

disprove: contradict
withholds: prevents
methinks: I think
mark: (here) listen to
but: (here) just
stood against: be heard
were disposed: wanted
parchment: document
testament: will
napkins: handkerchieves

Yea, beg a hair of him for memory,
And, dying, mention it within their wills,
Bequeathing it as a rich legacy
Unto their **issue**.

Fourth citizen We'll hear the will: read it, Mark Antony.

All The will, the will! We will hear Caesar's will.

Antony Have patience, gentle friends, I must not read it;
It is not **meet** you know how Caesar loved you.
You are not wood, you are not stones, but men;
And, being men, bearing the will of Caesar,
It will **inflame** you, it will make you mad:
'Tis good you know not that you are his heirs;
For, if you should, O, what would come of it!

Fourth citizen Read the will; we'll hear it, Antony;
You shall read us the will, Caesar's will.

Antony Will you be patient? Will you stay awhile?
I have **o'ershot** myself to tell you of it:
I fear I wrong the honourable men
Whose daggers have stabbed Caesar; I do fear it.

Fourth citizen They were traitors: honourable men!

All The will! The testament!

Second citizen They were villains, murderers: the will!
Read the will.

Antony You will **compel** me, then, to read the will?
Then make a ring about the corpse of Caesar,
And let me show you him that made the will.

How would the crowd behave if they heard the will?

bequeathing: saying in a will that you want somebody to have your wealth after you die

issue: (here) children

meet: (here) appropriate

inflame: make (you) angry

o'ershot: gone too far

compel: force

About the author

William Shakespeare (1564–1616) is considered one of the greatest poets and playwrights of all time. He wrote about 38 plays and 154 sonnets. Shakespeare's plays remain highly popular today and are studied, performed and reinterpreted in different cultural and political contexts throughout the world. Some of his other widely performed plays are *Macbeth*, *Hamlet* and *Romeo and Juliet*.

Comprehension

Quick Recap

A. Answer the questions in a few lines.

1. Where does the scene take place?
2. Who was asked to lead out one part of the gathered crowd to another street?
3. What did Brutus say would be given to the crowd?
4. Whom did the second citizen wish to hear? What would he do afterward?
5. To whom did Brutus address his speech? What would be Brutus' answer to anyone who asked him why he killed Caesar?
6. Who was given the permission to speak after Brutus?
7. How did Antony begin his speech? What did he refer to the conspirators as?
8. What did Antony mention about Caesar that made the crowd curious?

B. Answer the questions with reference to context.

1. *As Caesar loved me, I weep for him;*
   as he was fortunate, I rejoice at it; as he was
   valiant, I honour him: but, as he was ambitious,
   I slew him.
   a. Explain the given extract.
   b. What was Brutus trying to explain?
   c. Explain the line spoken by Brutus earlier, 'Not that I loved Caesar less, but that I loved Rome more.'
2. *The evil that men do lives after them;*
   The good is oft interred with their bones;
   So let it be with Caesar.
   a. Identify the speaker. What did he mean by 'The evil that men do lives after them'?
   b. Give two instances of Caesar's goodness that the speaker mentioned.
   c. How does the speaker use irony in this speech?
3. *Let but the commons hear this testament—*
   Which, pardon me, I do not mean to read—
   a. Who is the speaker in these lines? What did he claim to find?
   b. What was the reaction he expected from his audience if he read out the will?
   c. What surprising fact did he reveal from the will?

Life Skills and Values power of words, friendship and loyalty

Think and answer.

1. What was Brutus' motive for giving his speech? How was Antony's motive different from Brutus'?
2. Who, in your opinion, was the better orator—Brutus or Antony? Give reasons for your answer.
3. What, according to you, was the main quality of the citizens of Rome? Give examples to support your answer.

HC Participating in society – helping in maintaining systems

Way with Words

IRONY

You know how **irony** can be used to mean the opposite of what one says for greater dramatic effect.

Example: Brutus is an honourable man.

A. Explain the irony in the following situations.

1. A minister's son leads a protest march against the government.
2. Jason is a school bully. But he goes to sleep only when his mother tucks him in with his favourite toy.
3. Romeo and Juliet fell in love. Their parents were great enemies.
4. A weatherman organises a family picnic. As the family sets out, a thunderstorm breaks out.
5. Dying of thirst at sea, the ship's crew cried, 'Water, water, everywhere,/Nor any drop to drink.'

ARCHAIC SENTENCES

B. Rewrite these lines from the scene in contemporary English.

1. The noble Brutus is ascended: silence!
2. I pause for a reply.
3. I do entreat you, not a man depart,/Save I alone.
4. As I slew my best lover for the good of Rome, I shall have the same dagger for myself, when it shall please my country to need my death.
5. We are blessed that Rome is rid of him.

Grammar in Use

SIMPLE, COMPOUND AND COMPLEX SENTENCES

You have learnt that there are three types of sentences, based on structure.

A **simple sentence** has a subject and a finite verb. It has an independent clause.

Example: I will hear Cassius.

A **compound sentence** has two or more independent clauses, connected by a coordinating conjunction.

Example: Do grace to Caesar's corpse, **and** grace his speech.

A **complex sentence** contains a main clause and at least one subordinate clause, which is dependent on the main clause for meaning.

Example: He hath brought many captives home to Rome/**Whose ransoms did the general coffers fill.**

Here, the first part of the sentence is the main clause, while the words in bold form the subordinate clause.

A. Write whether these sentences are simple, complex or compound. Then, rewrite them according to the instructions given.

1. He sold his father's house. (begin: He sold the house that ...)
2. A dead man has no worries. (use 'who')
3. Buy two ties and get one free. (begin: If ...)
4. He tried his best but did not succeed. (use 'though')
5. He liked what I suggested. (use 'suggestion')
6. John admitted his guilt. (use 'guilty')
7. The clown entered the stage and the crowd started cheering. (begin: When ...)
8. Cancer is often curable and everyone knows it. (use 'that')
9. His deeds indicate his innocence. (use 'innocent')
10. When the detective arrived, the thief lost his nerve. (begin: Upon the arrival ...)
11. We lost the deciding match of the tournament. (use 'decide')
12. The ogre, who was captured, was actually a prince. (begin: The captured ...)

JOINING SENTENCES WITH CORRELATIVE CONJUNCTIONS

Correlative conjunctions are used in pairs to join two independent clauses.

Some commonly used correlative conjunctions are *either ... or, neither ... nor, as ... as, as much, as many, both ... and* and *no sooner ... than.*

Examples: **Either** Caesar was ambitious **or** Brutus was lying.
In this sentence, the correlative conjunctions express the probability of two options – that of Caesar being ambitious or Brutus lying.

Neither did Caesar accept the crown on the feast of the Lupercal **nor** did he keep the money from his conquests for himself.
In this sentence, the correlative conjunctions indicate the two actions that did not happen – acceptance of the crown and hoarding the money from the conquests.

Antony was **not only** a friend of Caesar **but also** an effective orator.
This sentence tells us that Antony was a friend as well as an effective orator.

B. Join the following sentences using appropriate correlative conjunctions.

1. Charlie loves football. Lola likes football.
2. It did not rain. The temperature did not come down.
3. You can go for the movie. You can stay at home.
4. He was an excellent cricketer. He was also good at his studies.
5. He began to eat lesser amounts. He also skipped meals.

Study Skills

Use Your Dictionary

William Shakespeare coined approximately 2000 words and phrases.
Example: In *Julius Caesar*, a character says 'It was Greek to me'. This phrase is now commonly used to mean that we do not understand something.

A. Here is a list of such words used in *Julius Caesar*. Use a dictionary to write their meanings and state the part of speech for each.

1. betimes
2. carrion
3. character
4. envy
5. fashion
6. gamesome
7. palter
8. prodigy

Pronounce Well

You know that the meanings of words can change depending on the stressed syllable. The meaning of a sentence can also change depending on the word that is stressed.

B. Listen to the the following sentence being read aloud in four ways, with stress laid on the word in bold each time. Note how the meaning changes each time. Then, practise saying it aloud in class.

1. **Let** him go up into the public chair. (Allow him to go up into the public chair.)
2. Let **him** go up into the public chair. (Only the designated person is allowed.)
3. Let him go **up** into the public chair. (He should go up, from where he could be heard and seen properly.)
4. Let him go up into the **public** chair. (He should go up to the designated place.)

C. Say these sentences aloud twice, laying stress on a different word each time. Write the meaning for each.

1. Everyone was there.
2. How did you know he was my friend?
3. Why don't you answer my question?
4. I like coffee more than tea.
5. You call this fresh orange juice?

Listening and Speaking

Enact the scene you have just read. Select the students who would play the major characters and act out the dialogue with proper expressions.

Pen it Down

A. Write a speech you have been asked to make on the occasion of the farewell of a much-respected teacher in your school.

You can include the following points in your speech:

- contribution of the teacher to the school
- your memories of the teacher
- what you have learnt from him/her

B. Imagine that Mark Antony wants to address the citizens of Rome separately to talk to them about the death of Caesar. Write a notice asking the citizens to gather at the forum, mentioning the date and time.

You can include the following points in the notice to draw the public's attention:

- the revelation of the contents of Caesar's will
- the real motive behind killing Caesar
- the names of the killers

Self Assessment

Now I can

- appreciate one of the greatest tragedies written by William Shakespeare.
- compare the styles of oratory of Brutus and Mark Antony, and the effect each has on the listeners.
- practise the transformation of simple, compound and complex sentences, and join sentences with correlative conjunctions.
- enact a scene from a play, write a speech and a notice on a given topic.

Research and Write

A. In 'A Short Walk in the Hindu Kush', the writer and his friend travel to Afghanistan to climb a remote mountain.

How has the nature of travel changed with technology, including the invention of trains, aeroplanes and more significantly, the Internet, which helps us connect with people across the world?

Prepare a presentation on the topic and share it with your class.

B. The poem 'The Last Wolf' describes a world in which the once common animal is on the brink of extinction.

Read the well-known science fiction novel *Do Androids Dream of Electric Sheep?* by Philip K. Dick, one of whose themes is the extinction of animals. In the book, owning live animals—which are very rare—is seen as a status symbol.

Discuss the similarities and the differences in the way the theme has been treated in the novel and the poem.

C. You read about the plight of the refugees in the poem 'Refugee Blues'. However, there are positive instances as well when refugees have endured hardships, fled from their homelands and then built their lives anew. Some such people went on to become a part of the Refugee Olympic Team, and participated in the Tokyo 2020 Olympic Games.

Read the following information on some famous refugee Olympians.

Name	Sport	Country of origin	Country of residence
1. Yusra Mardini	swimming	Syria	Germany
2. James Nyang Chiengjiek	track and field	South Sudan	Kenya
3. Masomah Ali Zada	cycling	Afghanistan	France
4. Popole Misenga	judo	Republic of Congo	Brazil

Now, work in groups and mark each athlete's country of origin and their current residence on a world map. Trace the distance covered by them, and find out how they made the perilous journey across countries. Discuss the adversities faced by each athlete in class.

D. Which, do you think, is more important: the individual or the greater good? Brutus sacrificed his friendship with Julius Caesar because he thought his loyalty to Rome was more important. Do you think he should instead have warned Caesar about the plot to assassinate him? What would you do if you were in his place?

Write an essay on the topic, giving reasons for your choice.

Literary Genres and Terms

Literary genres

Literary narratives can be of various kinds based on their style and form. The texts which you have read in this book are of various types. The following are some common types of narratives:

Prose

A **fantasy** is a story or novel which has a strange or other-worldly setting or characters. It often involves magic and supernatural creatures.

An **adventure** is a type of story or novel which has a lot of action and involves danger, risk and excitement.

Humour is a type of literature whose aim is to entertain people or make them laugh. A humorous story often has fun and excitement as its main elements.

A **fable** is a story about supernatural or extraordinary creatures, with a moral lesson at the end. In fables, animals, plants and non-living things often speak as humans.

A **fairy tale** is a story involving magical events and imaginary creatures like fairies, elves and goblins.

Science fiction is a type of story or novel about events set in the future or on other planets. They often involve future scientific progress, space, time travel and changes in the environment.

A **short story** narrates imaginary events and is usually only a few pages long.

A **folktale** is a story or myth handed down by word of mouth. Folk tales form part of the culture of a people, and can be based on superstitious beliefs.

A **legend** is a popular story about a particular person or place, handed down from earlier times and often believed to be true. A legend may be based on fact but may also include imaginary elements.

Mystery is a genre of fiction that deals with the solution of a crime or the uncovering of secrets.

Mythology are traditional stories relating to gods and were used by people for explaining various natural occurrences.

A **non-fiction** is a type of prose that is based on real events rather than imaginary ones.

A **novel** is a long prose narrative that deals with human experiences in an imaginative way. It has a plot which charts the journeys of its various characters, and also explores their personalities in detail.

An **autobiography** is an account of a person's life written by that person herself/himself.

A **biography** is the story of a person's life, written by someone else.

Horror is a type of story or a piece of writing which scares or startles the reader. A horror story creates a frightening atmosphere and often has supernatural themes and characters, like ghosts, witches and vampires.

A **parable** is a short story that teaches a moral lesson. Some of the best-known parables are the ones Jesus Christ told his disciples. Unlike fables, the characters in a parable are human beings.

Wildlife literature is writing related to the way animals and birds live in their natural habitat.

A **travelogue** is an account of the places a traveller has visited. It gives a glimpse into the life and culture of people who live in other—often remote—parts of the world.

An **allegory** is a narrative with two levels of meaning. The events and characters in the plot stand for abstract ideas and principles. An allegory usually aims to teach a moral lesson.

Historical fiction is a narrative that borrows real characters and events from the past. True events from history and imaginary tales are mixed together in historical fiction.

A **diary entry** is a record kept by a person in her/his diary. Diary entries are often personal and give insights into a person's thoughts and life that are otherwise not known to the public.

Poetry

A **lyric poem** is a short poem whose main purpose is to express emotions or a state of mind. It does not depict actions or events, as narrative poems do.

A **narrative poem** is a type of verse which tells a story. It often has the voices of the characters in the story, along with the narrator's voice.

Light verse is humorous poetry, usually dealing with playful themes and aimed at amusing the reader. It often uses literary devices, especially puns and alliterations.

A **nonsense poem** is a light-hearted, rhyming poem, often for young people, with peculiar characters in unusual situations or an unusual way of describing everyday things.

Free verse is a type of poetry which does not have a rhyme scheme. It is often written in the way people speak in daily life.

A **ballad** is a narrative poem that tells a story through dialogue and actions and is often set to music. These were originally written for dances.

A **sonnet** is a form of poetry consisting of fourteen lines. The first stanza, called octet, has eight lines and the second stanza, called sestet, has six lines.

A **dramatic monologue** is a poem in the form of a speech by a single person. The narrator is understood to be a person other than the poet. The presence of other people in the poem are only evident when the narrator addresses them.

An **ode** is a type of poem that is addressed to a particular person or object. Odes generally have irregular metre.

Drama

Drama is a type of literature that narrates a story which is meant to be acted out for an audience. There are two main types of drama: tragedy and comedy.

A **tragedy** is a play in which the central character faces misfortune and disaster. It often ends with the death or downfall of the character.

A **comedy** is a play with a light or humorous tone where the characters overcome difficult circumstances at the end. A comedy may not always be comical, that is, it may not be about amusing people or incidents.

Literary Terms

Authors and poets use various techniques to convey the meaning to their readers. These techniques are called literary terms. The following are some of the literary terms you have come across in the book:

A **simile** is a figure of speech in which someone or something is compared to a very different person or thing using 'as' or 'like'. **Example:** He is as brave as a lion.

A **metaphor** is a figure of speech in which a person or thing is compared to another, otherwise unrelated person or thing by stating that they are the same in a particular way. **Example:** She is a rose.

Personification is a way of imagining non-living things or abstract ideas as human beings with thoughts, actions and emotions. **Example:** The moon danced over the water.

Alliteration is a figure of speech in which the same consonant sound is repeated in consecutive or closely-placed words in the same sentence. **Example:** Slithering snakes slither silently through the grass.

Onomatopoeia is the use of words whose pronunciation is similar to the sounds they represent. **Example:** honk, bang, buzz

Exclamation is a figure of speech which is used to draw attention to something in a way that a simple statement cannot. It is used to express surprise, strong emotion or pain. **Example:** How tall the mountain is!

Irony is a figure of speech in which the real meaning is exactly the opposite of what is said. **Example:** Oh, what a lovely day! (said when it is cold and raining)

A **pun** is a literary device which plays on the different meanings of the same word, or the similar sound of different words, to produce a humorous effect. **Example:** Without geometry, life is pointless.

A **rhetorical question** is a question to which no answer is expected. It is asked in order to encourage the listener to consider a message or a viewpoint. **Example:** 'Aren't you ashamed of yourself?'

Hyperbole is a figure of speech in which the writer exaggerates and makes something sound bigger or more impressive than it really is. **Example:** 'I told you a thousand times!'

Euphemism is a literary device in which an unpleasant thing or sensitive topic is described in a way that makes it more acceptable. **Example:** 'He passed away' is a euphemistic way of saying 'He died.'

A **run-on line** is a literary device used in poems where a sentence runs on to the next line. The full meaning of the sentence can be understood only by reading the two lines together. **Example:** Lord, please give some sense of direction to this beetle/Who keeps blundering through the open window/And falling into the goldfish bowl.

Imagery is a literary device where descriptive language is used to help the reader imagine the world described in the narrative. It appeals to the five senses. **Example:** A burning forehead, and a parching tongue.

Repetition is a literary device where the same word or phrase is repeated at intervals to emphasise a particular idea. **Example:** But I have promises to keep,/And miles to go before I sleep,/And miles to go before I sleep.

Transferred epithet is a literary device where an adjective is placed beside a noun other than the one it is actually qualifying. It shifts the qualities of a person to an inanimate object. **Example:** He has spent a sleepless night.

Synecdoche is a literary device where a part of something is used to represent the whole and vice versa. **Example:** She stared at the faces which were hurrying along.

Metonymy is a literary device where an object that is not actually a part of something but is closely associated with it is used for referring to that object. **Example:** Let me give you a hand with the work. (Here, 'hand' means 'help.')

Climax is a literary device where words, phrases and sentences are arranged in the order of increasing importance to lead to a peak dramatic moment. **Example:** I came, I saw, I conquered.

Apostrophe is a literary device in which the speaker breaks away from the present scene to address an imaginary person or object. **Example:** Death, be not proud, though some have called thee/Mighty and dreadful.